# cigar cool

# cigar cool

jonathan futrell + lisa linder

cigars: people, places, and pleasures

*CLB*

This edition published 1999 by CLB,
an imprint of Quadrillion Publishing Limited,
Godalming Business Centre, Woolsack Way,
Godalming, Surrey, GU7 1XW, England.

Distributed in the US by
Quadrillion Publishing Inc.,
230 Fifth Avenue, New York, NY 10001.

First published in the UK 1998
as *Up in Smoke* by Conran Octopus,
a division of Octopus Publishing Group Ltd

ISBN 1-84100-314-X

Printed in China

# contents

**i**n what must be the rehabilitation phenomenon of the century, cigars are back—and big business.

While anti-smoking forces in Europe and the U.S.A. have cigarettes on the run, cigars have neatly sidestepped the attacks, returned from the sales slump of a decade ago, and emerged largely unscathed—not just more popular than ever, but a necessary decadence.

For the first time in the history of cigar smoking, what was once the parodied face of affluence is now a symbol of refinement, albeit with a dash of humor. What the personal organizer was to the 1980s, and the mobile telephone was to the 1990s, the hand-rolled cigar is to the second millennium—an essential part of the good life for those prepared to enjoy it.

Actors, rock-and-roll icons, designers, fashion models, and other members of the new glitterati have taken to cigars in a big way, and most are more than happy to put up their hand and be photographed, their new-found passion poised tantalizingly close to their lips. Their faces stare out at us from covers of magazines, published to foster and promote the cigar phenomenon we set out to explore here.

From Paris to Los Angeles, and from London to Havana, photographer Lisa Linder and I have met people with an unbridled passion for cigars and life. Musicians and film directors, media commentators and designers regaled us with tales of their favorite smokes; how they harbored their secret desire for years, only outing themselves recently, thanks to the new social acceptability of cigars. We spoke with the people who market and sell them, and we sat and smoked in the clubs, or divans, where cigar people retire at the end of the day.

We traveled to developing world Dominican Republic, risking life and limb in a rental car without brakes, to discover how the Young Turks are modernizing production and coping with demand. And finally, we went to Cuba to meet the people, touch the soil, and breathe the warm tropical air which together form the source of cigar mythology.

In a peculiar way our journey resembled meeting members of an unofficial, worldwide club, a sort of secret society dedicated to pleasure. Everyone seemed to know—or at least know of—the person we had spoken with days before, in another continent. Even if they had never met, each knew of the other's reputation: of their particular function in the global community of cigars. Through a world of elegant bohemians with a taste for tobacco, we were able to embrace and enjoy the traditions and rituals of cigars.

But it is not all lip-gloss and attitude; sales figures speak for themselves. From the start of the cigar boom in the early 1990s we have witnessed a fourfold increase in the world's appetite for premium hand-rolled cigars, whether from Cuba or elsewhere.

We are not dealing here with inexpensive, factory-rolled "short-fill" cigars, more often than not made with the tobacco that premium cigar makers reject. (Open one up and the insides consist of shavings.) The modern passion is almost exclusively for genuine, hand-rolled cigars. Pull one of those beauties apart and you will find whole tobacco leaves running the entire length to facilitate a smooth, unimpeded flow of smoke. They are wrapped and bound in more leaves, cultivated with diligence and care by farmers who understand the complex relationship between natural forces and flavor, then rolled in factories by nimble hands, in a process that has barely changed for centuries. Who could fail to be seduced by that?

As habits go, puffing on cigars is not a cheap one to sustain, especially if your fancy is for one of the revered Cuban brands. Yet, like the oenophile, unable to shake off a thirst for rare Burgundian wine, so the true devotee is prepared to pay handsomely for a box of genuine Havanas. Nevertheless, cigar production is booming in the Dominican Republic, Honduras, Nicaragua, Jamaica, and elsewhere in the tropics, and just as wine drinkers have adapted to New World blends, so the cigar lover is learning to embrace a different-and invariably cheaper-kind of smoke.

New cigar factories have opened in many countries while, across the globe, the retail side of the industry has experienced a corresponding expansion and, with that, the emergence of another phenomenon—the cigar club.

Cigar smokers are a breed apart; they enjoy the ritual of cigars (cutting, charring, lighting, smoking—talking cigars, too) and places like The No.1 Cigar Club in London, Cibar in New York, the Grand Havana Room in Los Angeles, and Cheroots in Kuala Lumpur are havens for lovers of this absorbing new passion.

Clearly the cult of the cigar is here. It is looking good, and it is in excellent company. **JF**

# the holy grail

# Nothing brings out the best in Cubans quite so convincingly as a good cigar.

Making your way through customs at Havana's Jose Marti Airport, the smell of tobacco is the first thing that hits you, after the distinctive slap of moist Cuban heat. Our taxi driver has a stogie pressed into his face for the entire duration of the drive into downtown Havana. We pass motorcyclists, old men watching the day, and a policeman changing the wheel of his squad car—each one is smoking a cigar.

This is a special day. Cigar people from all over the world are gathering at the Habana Libre Hotel for the annual Cigar Festival week. It's the cigar world's equivalent of the Academy Awards, where aficionados are invited to enjoy three of the year's finest smokes.

TV crews trip over themselves, searching for the famous, chasing actor Matt Dillon to his seat at the front of the stage; old friends, colleagues, and rivals in the cigar business back-slap and outdo each other with impressive custom-rolled stogies.

The national cigar company, Habanos, uses these dinners to reward success and launch new brands. Tonight the main feature is the Trinidad Fundador, a cigar roughly the same size as a Cohiba Lancero, at 7½in. long, but a little thicker, with a ring gauge of 40. It has never previously been for sale and, it was said, was only produced in limited numbers as a diplomatic gift. Some government voices had even denied its existence. However, with many major Cuban brands registered with powerful U.S.A. corporations who are ready to pounce if the trade embargo is lifted, the decision was taken to make Cuba's most mysterious cigar available to the general public, and launch it in typical flamboyant style.

Another of today's objects of desire is the Cuaba. A strange-looking beast, tapered at both ends, it was designed specifically for the British market and made to resemble the cigars of the 19th century. But it is the third choice that catches my eye, the Vegas Robaina, a cigar brand with the unique distinction of being named after a living Cuban. Such a tribute is unprecedented and would have been unthinkable in earlier revolutionary times, but things are changing fast in Cuba and the rules are being broken all the time.

robaina

So Vegas Robaina is the
brand, and Robaina himself
(pictured left) is now at center
stage, graciously receiving the
Tobacco Grower of the Year
award. He's a small, frail, 80-
year-old man, with white cropped
hair and skin like caramelized
parchment; his words of grati-
tude are drowned out by
applause. He bows and leaves.

To discover the reason for
such adulation and to try to
unravel some of the secrets, the
myths, and the hearsay of Cuban
tobacco production, we set out
the next day in a rental car,
equipped with the most basic
tourist map of the country, and
head west to Pinar del Rio.

Havana's suburbs around
Miramar, en route to the motorway,
look like Beverly Hills in need
of garden maintenance-modernist
and hacienda-style homes, avenues
of palm trees, and walls thick
with bougainvillea. In old
Havana, 19th-century homes are
collapsing in the middle of the
night from years of neglect, but
out here all is elegant and
secure; the soldiers on every
drive see to that.

Cuba is 777 miles from east to west and 119 miles at its widest, from north to south, and it boasts five tobacco-growing regions: the Vuelta Abajo, the Semi Vuelta, Partidos, Remedios, and Oriente. Each region produces a high quality of tobacco that other countries can only observe with envy. Yet only one, the Vuelta Abajo, in the region of Pinar del Rio, about three hours' drive southeast of Havana, produces leaves for all three component parts of the basic hand-rolled Cuban cigar (see page 34). This is the Côte Rôtie of the Rhone Valley, the Manzanilla of sherry; it is the source of Havana's finest; the Holy Grail. Here the soil is a livid hue of terracotta and for the cultivation of cigar tobacco, the combination of temperature and prevailing winds is unrivaled anywhere in the world.

If you want to be sure of growing the best tobacco for the finest cigars, you need a farm in the Vuelta Abajo, as close to the city of Pinar del Rio, in the province of the same name, as possible. Naturally, this is where you will find Alejandro Robaina.

The drive east, across a flat, uneventful land toward the Rosario Mountains, is remarkable for many things, not least the almost total absence of traffic in either direction. Bare-backed teenagers ride mopeds on the wrong side of the road; groups of hitchhikers are huddled beneath unfinished bridges leading to nowhere; and every mile or so, smiling farm workers wave at us with fronds of fresh garlic. We don't buy but they seem content with a wave in return.

From the terrace of the Los Jazmines Hotel, an elaborate pink edifice to the north of Pinar del Rio, at Vinales, we begin to sense the excitement most aficionados experience when first laying eyes on these tobacco fields. It is one of the most beautiful sights I have ever seen: serene and bountiful, a craggy valley of verdant granite monuments, towering above tobacco farms, and a portrait of Cuban life that can barely have changed for hundreds of years.

It is February, and midway through the harvest. Tobacco plants throughout the Vuelta Abajo are tall and succulent. People toil in almost every field we pass. Milky white oxen draw sleds of picked leaves and now and then we come upon dark-skinned men on horseback, their faces shaded by wide brimmed hats. Each one is smoking a cigar. The only buildings for as far as we can see are *casas del tabacos*, the pitch-roofed drying sheds.

Taking the road to San Luis, we had been told to turn left at the brow of the first hill, on to the dirt road, by a sign that read "Bien Venedo a la CCS VietNam Heroico" (Welcome to the Heroes of Vietnam Cooperative).

We follow this bumpy track into a valley and around past a a flamboyan tree or royal poinciana, bearing long dangling seed pods. Children and old folk emerge from wooden shacks to watch us bump and clank past their homes. Another flamboyan tree, some giant cacti, and discarded oil drums—and as we approach, chickens disperse in a fright of feathers. We press on through a broken-down car-repair yard, where both engines and buildings lie dead in the heat. Then right at a schoolhouse, through an avenue of tobacco, and into Vegas Robaina.

For such a living legend, Don Alejandro Robaina leads a humble existence. The land has been in his family since his grandfather bought it in 1845 and he personally took over the running of the farm from his father in the 1940s. The single-story house is squat and basic;

a verandah on three sides leads on to shady rooms, their walls adorned with photographs of Robaina's five children.

Don Alejandro shares the house with his sister, Marise, and his two most prized possessions, a pair of antique wind-up gramophones and a stack of 78rpm records. Over there, a picture of Pope John Paul, here some glass ornaments. He offers me a *puros*, the cigar equivalent of moonshine, rolled by one of his farm hands that morning.

"A lot of people come here; they want to take a picture of themselves with me for a souvenir," he says. "There was an American actor who had been in seven films. He was a fat man but I don't remember his name. There are ambassadors from Canada and Nicaragua, others from Africa, and bankers from Spain."

Don Alejandro Robaina has been Cuba's top tobacco grower for almost two generations. His leaves are used by several prestige Habanos brands, including Cohiba, and they can be found inside or wrapped around most top-of-the-range double coronas. When Cuba's entire harvest was very nearly wiped out by blue mold in 1979, Don Alejandro's skill not only kept the mold at

# the key is in knowing when to pick the tobacco.
If the *veguero* picks too early the cigar will not be good and it is the same even a day too late.

bay, it even helped increase his yield. Since 1997, though, when the range of four Vegas Robaina cigars was launched amid a fanfare of publicity in Madrid, Cuba's old man of tobacco has become a bona fide celebrity.

"Che Guevara's brother came here, but the second time he came I couldn't receive him. I was too busy with visitors."

Fame suits him well. He is at the top of his profession, outspoken and proud, a maverick in a process that has hardly changed for five centuries.

"For me the key is in knowing when to pick the tobacco. If the *veguero* picks too early the cigar will not be good, and it is the same even a day too late. You have to take the leaf at the precise moment and it is not easy to know either. Why do you think I have all this white hair?

"The state has never interfered in the way I cultivate my tobacco. For example, I am the only farmer in Cuba not to use a plow and turn the soil upside down. Instead I use disks to cut the soil and preserve the vegetable layer of the land, as it has always been. I learned this from my father.

"He taught me never to break a leaf; they should be taken off complete and not damaged. And if you put too much fertilizer around the plant the leaf will burn, because when they move the land around the tobacco to remove the weeds, some of it lands on the leaf and the taste can be destroyed by the chemicals. Also, when you take off the flower, if you do it badly you will destroy the plant. So many things to remember...

"That is why I have had the best results of the country and I can prove it—in quality and quantity, setting new national and international records. The state used to plant tobacco 12 inches apart and now they will plant it 14 inches so the leaf will grow bigger. That is because this is how I grow it. Really, you have to go even bigger, you have to move the plants further apart for better leaves.

"This is why I think I deserve to have my name on a cigar. Other brands can't talk. Trinidad can't talk, H.Upmann can't talk, Cohiba can't talk. Not one of the other brands can talk. But Vegas Robaina can talk... the brand is alive and talking to you."

# It is our last night in Pinar del Rio and all I want to do is drink rum and smoke cigars.

"Five boxes of my cigars were sent to Fidel, each signed by me. He said to give them to the president of the Cuban parliament because he doesn't smoke anymore. Nowadays I know he talks a lot about me. He wants to cut me into pieces to make a lot of other men who can grow tobacco like me."

After a second cup of coffee Don Alejandro shows us around the farm, to the fields of *corojo*, covered in tent-like sheets of muslin to protect the treasured *capa* leaves, tended by men on stilts. Then to his newest *casa del tabaco*. There I meet Maria Louisa, one of several women who use long needles to sew together hands of eight leaves which are hung on poles, called *cujes*, to dry. She prefers it here in the shade rather than in the field and she works fast —perhaps aided by the glass of rum at her side—her fingers bound with strips of fabric for protection against the needle. On a good day she can sew as many as 10,000 tobacco leaves.

"You see, Robaina is made with a lot of love and a lot of tears," says Don Alejandro.

The journey back to Havana is the most fraught of my life. It is not enough that the highway is unlit at night and our rental car is without a main headlight, or that the roadside is crowded with hitchhikers. There is another, even more terrifying, hazard: cattle. After a day spent grazing there is nothing the cows of Pinar del Rio like more than to sleep awhile on the warm tarmac of the Autopista Habana, oblivious to the fact that, on average, so I'm told, a speeding car slams into the flank of a sleeping heifer at the rate of one a week.

But we have no choice. The cigar factories are concentrated in Havana and our appointment at El Laguito, home of the Cohiba and now the enigmatic Trinidad, is first thing in the morning. Praying that the local cows are all wide awake, I step on it.

Cuba's most lauded cigar, the Cohiba (not its best-seller though, that remains the Montecristo) has been produced at the El Laguito factory since the 1960s. According to legend, Fidel Castro was so enamored of the taste of the home-rolled variety, smoked by one of his security guards, he decided to establish the factory in an elaborate 1920s, Italianate mansion on the outskirts of Havana (formerly the home of an English sugarcane magnate). This way, he could enjoy them himself, as well as impress visiting dignitaries.

t he factory was created by our Commander in Chief
and it was made with the idea of giving jobs to women.

The President chose the sizes he enjoyed best—the lancero, the corona especiale and panatela—and had their creator and blender, Eduardo Ribera, supervise production. It seems only right that El Laguito should have been chosen to produce the Trinidad, the cigar that has usurped the Cohiba as the ultimate symbol of Cuban diplomatic courtesy.

El Laguito is unlike any other factory I know, in the accepted sense of the word. The lemon and verdigris walls, the coiled staircase, the ornate architraves and the tall, shuttered windows are more suggestive of the world of opera than of a means of production. With the exception of an elevator, to move the bales of tobacco, the mansion remains virtually unchanged from when it was built in the 1920s. Boxes are stacked high in echo-filled corridors and the blenders, sorters, rollers, labellers, color graders, packers, and supervisors work in rooms that were originally designed for sleeping or eating in. Seventy percent of the workers are women, some with stogies on the go, and the atmosphere is one of toil and gossip. Above all though, El Laguito feels happy.

"That is what they tell me," says Emilia Tamayo, director of El Laguito since 1994 and the first woman to gain control of a Habanos cigar factory. "This is a general feeling. All the foreigners who visit us have the same sensation. They talk about the happiness of the people they see here, the look of the workers...

"The factory was created by our Commander in Chief and it was made with the idea of giving jobs to women. I came to work here in 1975. Before then I was a housewife, but I wanted to work, to be useful. The house is the grave of the woman.

"All the rollers used to be women until 1994, when I became director and I started to include men among the rollers. I'm no feminist," she says, beaming. "I think that men also have the right to work too...

"We care about our workers. We try to make their lives happy and help them. Also, there is equal treatment between the directors and the workers. We are different kinds of bosses."

Perhaps El Laguito has scope for development because it is the jewel in the crown of Habanos cigar factories, and because it is away from the city center, in a semi-rural setting. Indeed, a new factory is to be built on land adjoining El Laguito and the range of brands and blends is to be extended.

"Very powerful reasons mean we must change and grow," says Emilia. "It is not a secret that we have legal problems with different brands of cigars. There are companies abroad who want to steal Cuban brands. So we need to bring new brands to the market that are our own and cannot be taken from us.

"I am proud of the Trinidad; nothing is going to take it away from me."

With the Trinidad and the six sizes of the Linea Classica Cohiba, Emilia Tamayo oversees the production of, arguably, the finest cigars in the world. Yet when the new, slightly milder Cohiba, the Linea 1492 blend, was introduced in 1992 in five sizes to mark the 500th anniversary of Columbus's discovery of tobacco (one for each century), production of this range was allocated to the

Partagas factory in the heart of old Havana. To the serious enthusiast this is hallowed ground: the place of origin of many of the world's best cigars.

Anarchy reigns on the sidewalk directly outside the Partagas factory, beneath the red neon sign. Workers and friends gather here for a smoke and a chat and cigar-vending hustlers hiss for your attention, pouncing on tourists with offers of discounts on famous brands that would shame a used-car salesman.

Most of the cigars on offer are either fake or stolen and only a fool would be tempted when unlimited stocks of the real McCoy are just a few steps away, on the ground floor of the Partagas cigar store.

Compared to El Laguito, Partagas is a real factory: noise and bustle, rattly service elevators stuffed with people and tobacco, students learning the ropes, heat and sweat, rows of cigar rollers in solitary contemplation of their task, and piles of cigars, all yearning to be smoked. Some shapes, like the vast Partagas Lusitanias double corona and the pyramid-shaped Montecristo No. 2 (a personal favorite), are familiar, while others like Solomon, an inflated figurado specially commissioned by a German customer, I could only marvel at.

# tobacco production

1. The basic hand-rolled Cuban cigar, the benchmark of all cigars, is the sum of three component parts, derived from two varieties of tobacco plants: the *criollo* and *corojo*.

The components are the *tripa* (filler) in the center; a *capote* (binder) around the *tripa* (both taken from the *criollo* plant); and a *capa* (wrapper) stretched and rolled around the outside (taken from the *corojo*).

Special growing conditions and superlative skills are required to produce the *capa*, the most prized leaf in any cigar.

2. Two varieties of seeds, from the *corojo* and *criollo* plants, are produced at government research stations and, once coated with a protective wax, distributed for planting.

Recently, two new disease-resistant seed strains have been planted: Habana 2000 and Habana 92.

From an October planting, it takes 50 days for plants to reach maturity. Tended daily, the plants' flowering heads and side shoots are removed to stimulate the growth of larger leaves.

3. *Criollo* plants are divided into three sections: The *volado* leaves, the oldest and mildest, nearest the base of the plant; the *seco* medium leaves in the center; and the most flavorsome, the youngest, *ligero* leaves, at the top.

*Corojo* plants are grown in fields beneath sheets of muslin, to protect the leaves from direct sunlight and to give them a lustrous, silken appearance, a process called *tapado* (or covering). Eight, sometimes nine pairs of leaves, each with a different name, color and taste, are picked separately, usually a week apart.

4. All harvested leaves are taken to drying barns, built facing east and west, to shelter their contents from the harmful midday sun. The temperature inside is carefully controlled.

Leaves are sewn into hands of eight and strung on poles (*cujes*) to dry. Air curing takes about 50 days.

The art of the tobacco blender is to combine the *volado*, *seco*, and *ligero* leaves with the correct binder and wrapper, to ensure flavor, texture, and good burning qualities.

Production of *corojo* is labor intensive and expensive. A good plant will wrap 32 cigars.

# cigar production

1. The leaves are stacked in three-feet-high *pilones* and stored at temperatures not exceeding 95°F. Fermentation breaks down resins and creates uniformity of color.

Leaves are graded for size and color before a second fermentation. The temperature is checked with sword-like thermometers.

After resting for three weeks, the leaves are packed into bundles called *tercios* and put aside for a few months in the cigar factories for aging.

2. Prior to rolling, the leaves are gently separated and, in bunches, lightly moistened with high-pressure water.

*Despalilladoras* remove the stems and *rezagadoras* grade the remaining half leaves into size, color and texture.

The filler comprises three types of leaf (*volado*, *seco*, and *ligero*), and throughout the process blenders monitor the progress of each.

Once perfected they are taken to the *liga* (the blending room), where great secrecy surrounds the individual cigar blends.

3. *Torcedores* (rollers) sit at benches, six or more to a row, using a *chaveta* (half-moon blade) and a wooden board.

Two to four leaves are combined with the binder and rolled into a bunch, according to the blend.

After pressing in a wooden mold they are wrapped, trimmed, and capped using leaf and natural gum.

A good *torcedore* rolls from 120 to 150 cigars a day. These are gathered into bundles of 50 and checked by quality controllers.

4. After rolling, the cigars are placed in conditioning rooms for up to three weeks for the flavors to marry.

Some of the highest paid and respected factory workers are *escogedores* (color graders). Working at phenomenal speeds they grade the cigars according to color (65 shades in all) and texture. Others arrange them in boxes from dark to light from left to right.

Cigars are removed from the boxes, for banding, by women *anilladoras*, using a simple measuring rule and gum.

# Workers and friends gather here for a smoke and a chat and cigar-vending hustlers hiss for your attention, pouncing on tourists with offers of discounts on famous brands that would shame a used-car salesman.

Right: Havana mechanic Sergio Morales:
"Like cigars, Harleys are part of my family life."

Located deep in the dark, steaming basement is a tobacco fermentation room; the aroma is stifling. On the first floor I encounter Hilda Chacon, a tobacco grader, who rolls herself a cigar the size of a baseball bat each day when she arrives, wedging the soggy end firmly into her mouth where her front teeth used to be.

If Cuba is to continue to increase its cigar production, new rollers are needed. Ernesto, who is 18, is one of two dozen trainees at Partagas, most still in their teens, who are grappling with the intricacies of rolling. Their target is 150 cigars a day; after seven months, Ernesto is still only on 120. Each trainee is provided with a wooden rolling block and *chaveta*, a half-moon blade.

"It is difficult to get on the course. There is a lot of competition and it is hard work," he says. "Speed is one thing—it is very important—but the skill lies in combining that with quality, so that each cigar looks and feels and smokes like the last."

He is learning to roll Partagas corona grandes and laughs out loud at the thought of his first attempt. "It was a fifth of the quality I can roll now. You could barely smoke it."

# he is learning to roll Partagas corona grandes

and laughs out loud at the thought of his first attempt. "It was a fifth of the quality I can roll now. You could **barely smoke it**."

In the top-floor cigar-rolling room of Partagas, a room, like all the others, painted pistachio and brown, I meet Santiago Garcia Perez, a man with a remarkable resemblance to the late Miles Davis. When I offer this observation, he insists he is, in fact, the spitting image of Mahatma Gandhi.

Over the years, the role played at this and other cigar factories by this striking man, now in his seventies, has been crucial. Now retired, Don Perez was a reader whose job, for 50 years, was to read newspaper articles and novels to the workers. It is a service that began in the 1860s and continues to this day. It has even provided the names for top cigar brands: the names Romeo y Julieta and Montecristo are derived directly from two of the most popular stories read in the factories.

"The reader is the one who delivers information and spreads the news," says Don Perez, relighting his cigar. "What is read is not a decision of the reader though; it depends on what the rollers and the workers want to hear."

# What is read is not a decision of the reader; it depends on what the rollers and the workers want to hear.

"If they are sad, a reader would read something to make them happy—classical works of world literature. Or for information, they may want to be read to from different newspapers: from France, Spain, Russia, the Czech Republic, and England, too. Cubans want to learn it all. The reader is just the bearer of information—the topic is decided by the people —like the director of an orchestra," he says, through the haze of blue-gray smoke. He contemplates the imagery he has just conjured, and adds: "Ah, Cuban cigars, such a symphony!"

We had come to Cuba not really knowing what to expect. We had been warned about the bureaucracy by influential men who know Cuba well about the institutionalized slowness of the country and the way nothing ever gets done when, or how, you would like it.

But would I really have wanted it any other way? Whenever our best-laid plans were spoiled, someone would produce a cigar and a light, sometimes a glass of rum too, and then, believe me, Cuba was transformed into the most godly country on earth.

# spreading the seed

# Many exiled Cuban cigar makers took their original molds with them when they left Cuba under Spanish, and later Castro's, rule.

Right: Bunches of filler, rolled and held together with binder leaves, are placed into wooden molds and mechanically pressed. Once their shape is held, the outer wrapper leaf can be put on.

You are not born with a passion for cigars. Like all the best things in life, they demand patience and determination.

I got my first big chance at an early age... and blew it. My Uncle Ronnie, a journalist in London, had returned from an assignment in Cuba, then in the first flushes of revolution, and despite my tender adolescence, he stuffed a huge claro claro Havana cigar in my mouth and passed me the matches.

I recall its size vividly, and still half suspect that it was cigars such as this, and not nuclear warheads, that were at the heart of the Cuban missile crisis.

Here was an invitation to an exclusive club called manhood, and all I can remember was turning the same green as the cigar, and throwing up. I didn't care if I never saw another cigar again as long as I lived—until I discovered Eighth Street in Little Havana.

On any afternoon men in *guayaberas*—short-sleeved cotton shirts traditionally worn in the Caribbean—hang around hole-in-the-wall cafés, sipping syrupy black coffee from tiny plastic cups and smoking cigars in the casual way GIs chew gum. Noisy old men in Domino Park chomp their stogies into vile, oily stumps and there are so many cigar factories you can smell the sweet odor of tobacco on every corner.

It's the kind of place where anyone is happy to smoke a cigar, freewheeling and easy; where roast-pork smells blend with the sounds of syncopated Latin music.

I push past the brown door of the El Credito cigar factory, and at the small corner counter, in view of the lines of cigar rollers, purchase a pocketful of cigars in all shapes and sizes. Then, I take my place at the counter of the coffee shop on the opposite corner, and slowly and patiently cultivate a new passion in my life: not in the oak-paneled room of a gentleman's club, nor in the steps of Ernest Hemingway in Old Havana, but right here, on Eighth Street, Miami, Florida, U.S.A.

Cigars have been made and smoked in the U.S.A. since the 18th century, possibly earlier. Indeed it was a factory in Conestoga, Pennsylvania, that gave rise to the word "stogie."

The cigar makers from Cuba, with their special skills and sacks of prized Cuban seed, arrived later, in two waves: the first during Cuba's struggle for independence from Spain, in the late 18th century. Many leading tobacco growers and cigar makers established themselves in Key West and later, to a greater degree, in Ybor City, near Tampa. By the turn of the century there were 200 factories around Tampa, employing over 5,000 workers, nearly all of them Cuban.

In fact, if you should by some chance find yourself in Whippany, New Jersey, take a peek at J.R. Cigar's high-tech mailorder department. Using timbers and fittings from the original Ybor City factories, owner Lew Rothman has constructed a shrine to the founding fathers of the Cuban-American cigar tradition.

That first wave backed the uprising against Spain, and in 1895 Cuban hero José Marti (Havana's airport is named in his honor, and his statue stands in front of every Cuban school) led the re-invasion. Details of the attack were delivered to the resistance, rolled inside a cigar, of course.

The second wave arrived, fleeing the Cuban revolution of 1959 and wanting no part either of communism, or the Fidel Castro administration.

Left: Eric Milon, at The Living Room, believes South Beach is "like the Côte D'Azur with the American way."

# t

hey may not smoke as many cigars in Miami
as they do in New York, nor have as many uptown settings
to do it in, yet in many ways this tropical city
is much more of a cigar town.

The arrival of the second wave of Cuban cigar makers coincided with a decline in cigar consumption in the U.S.A., in preference for much cheaper, machine-made cigarettes Production in Ybor City was scaled down and, looking for work, some cigar blenders and rollers drifted south to Miami, establishing businesses, and a neighborhood, in Little Havana.

You will find local cigar stores in every shopping mall, and dozens of divans in and around heavily gentrified South Beach—the art deco district of Miami Beach—notably on Lincoln Road. Along Ocean Drive, girls sell cigars from trays while, a couple of blocks away, The Living Room nightclub host, Eric Milon, has installed a cigar vending machine. A world first!

"When the girl comes over, she has four or five cigars," explains Eric, above the din. "They can go from $8 a cigar to $30, like a wine list. The point is, you may not want to go up to her and ask for a cheap one... because the girl looks pretty and you don't want to look cheap yourself. No problem. Go to the machine, put the money in, and if you want a good cigar we have Cohibas, but if you want a less expensive cigar you can have it, and nobody will know."

There are more than 20 small, independently owned cigar factories in Little Havana and that number is growing. They include El Credito, the Caribbean Cigar Company, Caribbean Connection, and the inimitable Moore & Bode.

Unusually, Moore & Bode pay their rollers by the day, rather than by the "stick"; a small label is used on the cap of the cigar instead of a traditional band; and, in place of cedar boxes, cigars are dispatched in bundles, wrapped in aluminum foil and bubble-wrap. They also absolutely refuse to divulge where they buy their tobacco. If they are unable to get the tobacco they require for either of their two blends—Miami and Flamboyan—they simply do not make those cigars. Moore & Bode are purists, and proud.

"We are what could be described as highly eccentric," says owner Sharon Moore. "No fake Latin style; very straightforward, just clean classics."

"hundreds of cigar factories have
    closed in the Dominican Republic,
and eventually there will only
    be about 30 left," says Hendrik Kelner
of Davidoff. "The important thing
    for us is to maintain the reputation
we have worked hard since the
    1970s to establish, and I do not
want to see that eroded."

*i*am taken with the small scale of the operation—in a former corner store—and the diligence and warmth of the rollers, who look more like cafeteria workers than the conventional idea of cigar rollers: no exposed thighs here. But what really grabs my attention, and for me what sets Moore & Bode apart, is its top-of-the-range pyramid cigar: full brass. Shaped like an ice-cream cone, it is 7¼in. long with a 64 ring gauge.

"It's a beautiful cigar," says Sharon. "A resident of London, well known for his love of cigars, has some shipped to him from Boston every couple of weeks. For him, the full brass is an excellent mid-morning cigar. If this is his mid-morning cigar, where does he go from there?"

In fact, from a purely historical perspective, the full brass is effectively a more refined and better tailored version of the cigar Hilda Chacon rolls herself each morning, before she begins work at the Partagas factory in Havana. And that monster, in turn, is clearly a descendant of the *tabacos* that Christopher Columbus found the indigenous Indians smoking when he landed in Cuba in 1492.

At the time this encounter was chronicled by the monk Bartolome de las Casa:

"All the men carried a torch, breathing in the heady smoke like incense. A few dry herbs were placed on a dry leaf, which was then rolled up into a tube, not unlike a small musket barrel. This was then lit at one end. They inhaled a type of smoke from the other end with each breath, said to soothe the body and have a pleasant, inebriating soporific effect."

The Spanish role in the subsequent development of tobacco and cigar production cannot be overstated. It began with factories in the Canary Isles, and by the 18th century many more had been established throughout mainland Spain.

To this day, Spain remains the single largest importer of Cuban tobacco in the world and is the cheapest country in Europe, by far, in which to buy premium, hand-rolled Cuban brands. For these reasons, plus the fact that smoking is as much a part of the Spanish psyche as Catholicism, Habanos launched Alejandro Robainas'

Vegas Robaina range in Madrid in 1997 amid a publicity fanfare befitting royalty.

The Spanish tobacco company, Tabacalera Cigars International, has invested $367 million in a number of factories and cigar distribution companies in the United States, Honduras, and Nicaragua. It now controls 11 percent of the world market, with a stated ambition to be the biggest and most powerful cigar company in the world.

Tobacco is grown throughout the Caribbean, Central America, and the U.S. southeast, as well as in more unexpected states like Connecticut, Pennsylvania, and Wisconsin. Highly prized wrapper leaf is grown in the humid, foggy valleys of Ecuador, Java, and Sumatra and big investments are being made in the Philippines and Brazil. Cameroon is noted for its dark, sweet wrapper leaf, and new land is being made available to growers in India and China. In fact, Alejandro Robaina has been invited to China to advise on planting and production techniques.

It was not the communist revolution in Cuba per se that changed the face of tobacco and cigar production in the Caribbean, although many producers did flee Cuba during that period, taking their skills with them. Rather, it was the subsequent trade embargo—Cubans still tend to refer to it today as a "blockade"—imposed by President John Kennedy in 1962, which changed the industry forever. The big American corporations that had invested there, and many anti-Castro, independent cigar families, found themselves without a natural base to work from.

The effect of the embargo was to deny North Americans the cigars to which they had been accustomed for centuries, and simultaneously to boost investment and production in those neighboring Caribbean islands and parts of Central America that were already geared up for tobacco.

In many cases they used seed strains taken from Cuba during the post-revolution exodus. Mexico, Honduras, Ecuador, and recently Panama have all been beneficiaries. None, though, has profited from the embargo quite as dramatically as the Dominican Republic, situated just a few miles east of Cuba.

# Millions of North Americans have grown accustomed to the milder, smoother smoke from the Dominican Republic.

Formerly the island of Hispaniola, and now split between the Dominican Republic in the east and Haiti in the west, this verdant, tropical country is the world's biggest producer of premium hand-rolled and machine-made cigars: around 200 million "sticks," or nearly half the world market. The vast majority of this output is shipped to the U.S.A.

To many nonsmokers the Dominican Republic represents all that is wrong with beach resort vacations: scruffy, tacky, and with terrible food. Entire stretches of the north and south coasts are colonized by anonymous resorts, popular with German and British tourists, where indigenous culture has been reduced to gaily colored souvenirs.

The drive south across the Cordillera Mountains, to the city of Santiago de los Caballeros, is a welcome and heavenly contrast: blue-gray mountains as far as the eye can see and, in the near distance, palm-fringed hills. Along the way we pass through villages where old men give toothless grins and children stop to wave and pose for the camera.

No one could describe Santiago as beautiful. The grand Spanish colonial architecture is nearly all to be found further south, in Santo Domingo. Meanwhile, Santiago is anarchic and new, a developing world city full of traffic jams and fumes, dusty streets desperately in need of repair, and noisy bars. Cigar money is pouring in, much of it invested in shopping malls and multinational burger bars.

The true source of Santiago's wealth lies a short drive to the east, in the Cibao Valley: an idyllic rural backwater, bisected all the way from Santiago to Montecristi in the far northwest, by the Yaqui del Norte River. Hemmed in by mountains on either side, this is the Dominican Republic's version of Cuba's Vuelta Abajo, where, except for the unique orange topsoil, temperature, rainfall, and humidity are almost identical.

It could almost be Cuba. Which is why, for decades, growers have been able to duplicate the taste, strength, and aroma of Cuban tobacco. Havana devotees, mostly Europeans who have easy access to Cuban cigars, will say they have failed. However, millions of North Americans have grown accustomed to the milder, smoother smoke from the Dominican Republic.

# thousands of new acres have been planted in the Cibao Valley, and the rarest commodity of all is the cigar roller.

Left: Danny with leaves that will soon be rolled into Arturo Fuente cigars.

The basic process is the same, with subtle differences. Cibao Valley drying barns are lower and wider, some with thatched roofs, some without roofs at all, and some where growers use fires to dry the leaves. And instead of sewing the hands of leaves together, here they are tied into bunches with strips of palm leaf.

Ironically the population here does not have a tradition of cigar smoking; they prefer cigarettes. All production is restricted to tax-free, so-called free zones, from which all cigars are shipped directly to foreign markets. Yet, in the Cibao Valley I came across strands of leaves, strung out along the walls of shanty huts, a sign that things are changing. Perhaps ordinary Dominican Republicans want to discover what all the fuss is about and are having a try themselves.

The unprecedented demand in the U.S.A. for Dominican cigars has seen the number of factories rise from a couple of dozen at the start of the boom, in 1992, to around 250 at its height in 1997. Get-rich-quick entrepreneurs arrived in droves, creating blends and making deals with locals who had no experience in producing premium hand-rolled cigars. Before you knew it, the U.S.A.

was awash with cheap, sub-standard cigars.

Thousands of acres have been newly planted with tobacco in the Cibao Valley, and the most-prized commodity of all is the cigar roller. Rolling schools have been established to cater to the demand but factory owners report that their best rollers are frequently head-hunted; others work shifts in two, sometimes three factories.

The largest tax-free zone is a short drive north of downtown Santiago, past the airport and sports stadium, through a shanty town, and on the far side of a set of iron gates where uniformed men search cars and people for contraband. Inside this fence there are over 200 companies employing 40,000 people, producing anything from shoes to cosmetics. There are snack-vending carts on corners and impenetrable iron fences making staff canteens look like prison compounds.

I arrange to visit the American-owned General Cigar factory, where they make the DR Cohiba, Macanudo, and Partagas. Nothing remotely romantic here. The factory is run with soulless precision, far removed from anything we saw in Cuba: a large, open-plan workshop, with bales of tobacco entering at one end and boxes of hand-rolled cigars leaving at the other.

Just around the corner is one of the Arturo Fuente factories, the largest family-owned operation in the country. Don Arturo Fuente left Cuba during the Spanish war, establishing a cigar factory in Tampa. Since then his descendants have moved around the Caribbean—Honduras, Nicaragua, and Puerto Rico—dodging wars, revolutions, and political upheavals, before settling in the Dominican Republic in 1980.

From a small workshop with seven rollers, the Fuentes today have their own plantations and employ almost 2,000 rollers. Their success, primarily in the U.S.A., is down to a range of superb cigars standing head and shoulders above the competition for quality and flavor. The Fuente Opus X range is one of only a few sought-after Dominican Republic cigars, and the Fuentes family is now committed to growing all of its own wrapper leaf, a practice previously unheard of in the Dominican Republic, where, until now, all wrapper leaf has been imported.

My next appointment is at a factory partly owned by cigar legend Hendrik Kelner and the Swiss-based Davidoff empire, in another free zone a few miles away. This factory replaced an earlier one destroyed by fire in 1996. It is pristine and white, with the word "Davidoff" written in green scroll along the walls.

Hendrik Kelner has seen hundreds of get-rich-quick merchants arrive in the Dominican Republic, aiming to exploit the cigar boom in the U.S.A. They set up hundreds of new factories, (invariably lacking in the traditional skills of blending and production) and employ untrained rollers. Most ventures quickly turn sour, and many of the resultant cigars are left unsold on the shelves of American tobacconists. Kelner, sees one of his roles as improving the public perception of cigars from his country.

"Hundreds of factories have closed and soon there will only be about 30 left," explains Kelner. "The important thing for us is to maintain a reputation for quality. Since the 1970s we have worked hard for it and I do not want to see that eroded."

He hopes to achieve this with an association of Dominican Republic cigar producers who have introduced a gold seal of approval depicting tobacco leaves, the national flag, and the words *garantia de calidad*

Pages 68-71: Tobacco production in the Cibao Valley: the true source of Santiago's wealth.

—quality guaranteed—to be applied to all leading brands.

"Our other weapon is continually checking and blending," says Rene Hollenstein, a Davidoff man who has worked closely with Kelner. Davidoff has become a byword for quality control. Their cigars are monitored at eight stages during the production process, and Hollenstein smiles when I repeat the rumor that Davidoff rejects more cigars than it sells.

"We continually monitor and check. One way we do this is to smoke cigars made with just one of the three filler tobaccos. This shows us exactly how it would taste if we didn't blend. And believe me, it tastes terrible. The next cigar is made with the second tobacco from the final blend, and the third cigar the last tobacco.

"A fourth cigar contains the entire mixture and then we see exactly what the three components mean in your mouth: one tobacco dries it, the other hurts the tongue—it's too sweet, too salty—and the third is too bitter.

"A good blend will eliminate all the negative parts and only bring in the positive tastes." Like Don Perez, Hendrik calls it a symphony, "starting with the violins, then the drums and at the end, the trumpets."

Until the 1970s the cigar families who departed Cuba and started afresh elsewhere began with totally new brands. It must have seemed to them, since they no longer had access to genuine Cuban tobacco, that they had forfeited the right to use their former brand names. That was until an international court ruled that certain owners retained exclusive rights to their original names, in the U.S.A. and elsewhere.

Since then many brands formerly associated only with Cuba have been produced in the Dominican Republic and Honduras. Today there is a dual-nationality Cohiba, El Rey del Mundo, Hoyo de Monterrey, H.Upmann, Montecristo, Partagas, Punch Punch, and Romeo y Julieta. The big American tobacco conglomerates are marketing Cuba's cigar mythology, albeit in a different blend and from another country, to a generation of smokers who have not known anything else.

Cuba has responded with new brands of its own: Cuaba, Vegas Robaina, and Trinidad, with more certain to follow. Only they have the rights to these brands and, rightly or wrongly, nobody will be able to impersonate them.

# b
## and on the run:
# Davidoff
## spreads the seed.

March 1990. Shock waves reverberate around the international cigar trade. It is the day Davidoff, purveyor of fine Havana cigars for two decades, pulls out of Cuba and shifts its entire operation to the Dominican Republic.

Born in Kiev, and driven out of Russia by the pogroms, Zino Davidoff learned the tobacco trade in his father's shop in Geneva. He was one of the first aficionados to make a connection between cigars and wine, insisting that both may improve with age. By the end of World War II he had assembled an impressive stock of vintage Cuban cigars. In 1947 he launched his own Chateau collection of cigars, greatly influenced by the Cuban Hoyo de Monterrey brand.

In 1969 Cubatabaco invited Zino Davidoff to produce a range of Havanas bearing his name. The following year he went into partnership with Swiss cigar importer Ernst Schneider, and subsequently opened Davidoff stores in a number of major cities around the world.

Davidoff's decision to pull out of Cuba, citing poor quality control, and thereby dramatically altering the character and taste of his cigars, upset many customers. But, for all the brouhaha and calls of betrayal, Davidoff remains the biggest independent producer of premium cigars in the world. For sheer rolling perfection, presentation, and a balanced, albeit slightly milder flavor, the five Davidoff blends—Aniversario, Number series, Grand Cru, Mille, and Special—are hard to beat. Zino Davidoff built a global cigar empire of cigars and designer style, in everything from clothes to cognac. He died, aged 88, in 1994.

**i**f I am completely truthful I have to admit that I went to the Dominican Republic with a feeling, common among European smokers, that no matter how good a cigar may be, whether from here or any other country, if it is not Cuban it can only ever be second best.

A serious and extremely wealthy cigar collector in London once gave me a Fuente Opus X Reserva No. 1, a cigar many in the U.S.A. would cut off their right arm for. It was not necessarily intended as a generous gift; rather, it was the act of a man ridding his otherwise perfect Cuban collection of an unwanted growth.

Then I recall the marvellous cigar life in Miami: the mood of the streets, the music, the informal manner in which cigars are enjoyed. And I reach my own conclusion that a cigar's origin is of little significance. It is only the ingredients, the person who made it, and the person who is smoking it that really count. And if by some chance one of the three is Cuban? Well, so much the better, but nothing more.

# If I cannot smoke cigars in heaven, I shall not go.

JFK

Orson Welles

Elvis

Arnold Schwarzenegger

Nicholson

Clint Eastwood

Groucho Marx

James Belushi

John

Che Guevara

Alfred Hitchcock

Fidel Castro

Ava Gardner

Huston

Jack

Ernest Hemingway

Humphrey Bogart

# power & passion

# On stage Orson Welles

would use his cigar almost as others use a cane,
in a repertoire of jousting actions.

Sharon Stone (previous page) and Orson Welles (right):
the new cigarati and the old guard.

In a generation determined to stamp out vice of any kind, cigars are rapidly taking on the symbolism of the Alamo for the resolutely incorrigible. Anti-stogie forces are raging all around and yet, just as all seems doomed for tobacco lovers, another movie icon or supermodel raises a head above the parapet, declaring allegiance to the cigar. Passion or fashion, who can tell?

Nobody was unduly surprised to learn that Hollywood heavy-hitters Arnold Schwarzenegger and Danny DeVito enjoy them. A memorable incident some years ago saw Schwarzenegger being interviewed for *Playboy* magazine. He lit a cigar, then informed the journalist that the interview would terminate when the cigar was finished.

Eyebrows were raised, however, when Demi Moore owned up to a cigar habit. She smokes to unwind and is reported to possess a travel humidor, a gift from fellow cigar travelers Tom Cruise and Nicole Kidman, for the Cohibas she keeps in her trailer when filming. Moore has also been known to dress up in men's clothes and light up, an affectation previously adopted by Marlene Deitrich and the 19th-century French female novelist George Sand.

Actors Alec Baldwin, Pierce Brosnan, Matt Dillon, Sharon Stone, John Travolta, Isabella Rossellini, and Lauren Hutton have all gone public. In the film version of Paul Auster's *Smoke*, Harvey Keitel stars as the owner of a Brooklyn cigar store. The performance was authenticated by a real-life passion for cigars which Keitel shares with his friend and fellow actor Robert De Niro.

You only have to read the humidor brass plates in the more renowned cigar clubs to discover who is up in smoke. Those in the Grand Havana Room, Los Angeles, a cigar club for the Hollywood "cigarati," make for especially interesting reading.

the surest way of establishing your credentials as a romantic, with Latin blood running through your veins, is to smoke a cigar with connotations of Cuba and enjoy long hot humid nights beneath a ceiling of blue haze. That's how Ernest Hemingway played it. He sent Ava Gardner the band from the cigar he was smoking on the night they met.

# Challenged by a football referee as to what he was doing with a cigar in his mouth Groucho countered by asking: is there another way to smoke it?

Some enthusiasts have even been prepared to put their money and skills where their cigars are. *Blowing Smoke*, "a film about guys and cigars," according to club manager Stan Shuster, was shot in the Grand Havana Room. It's a joint project by several high-rolling members, including director/writers James Orr and Jim Cruickshank and actors Jim Belushi, Stephen Baldwin, Peter Weller, Kevin Pollack, Joe Pantoliano, and Joe Mantegna.

Orson Welles rarely went on stage without a cigar, and is even on record as saying that he purposely wrote cigar-smoking characters into his films just so that he could smoke for free. On stage, Welles would use his cigar almost as others use a cane, in a repertoire of jousting actions. On film, as the racketeer Harry Lime in Graham Greene's *The Third Man*, the smoke from his cigar became a sinister and haunting symbol of greed and immorality.

For comedians Groucho Marx and George Burns, puffing on a cigar was a carefully contrived act, allowing their audiences time to get the gags. Burns, who lived to be 100 years old and who often boasted that he outlived the doctor who told him to quit, has an imprint of his trademark cigar, right next to his hands, in the sidewalk outside Mann's Chinese Theater in Hollywood.

If Elvis Presley were alive today, he might have been among the first of the current crop of cigarati to go public. Back in the 1950s and 1960s, the image of the fat-cat cigar smoker was all-pervasive; cigars could not have been less cool. The King understandably maintained his passion for Havanas behind closed doors. He must have taken one look at director Alfred Hitchcock, rarely photographed without a cigar and bowler hat, and decided that that persona was definitely not for him.

The traditional image of the introspective cigar smoker is the epitome of self-containment and contentment. Lost in a state of grace, silent in contemplation, and enveloped in clouds of aromatic smoke, he inhabits a private place the outside world is unable to penetrate. In such circum-stances, momentous projects have been, and continue to be, conceived.

# murder, mystery, suspense, and a good cigar
## –the hallmarks of Alfred Hitchcock.

Meanwhile, the cigar-fueled contemplations of Ilich Ramirez Sanchez, otherwise known as Carlos the Jackal, have led to the deaths of at least 83 people. Currently serving a 30-year prison sentence, the 48-year-old terrorist, formerly the world's most wanted man, describes himself as a "professional revolutionary." He revealed his passion in a letter to French magazine *L'Amateur de Cigare*. As a subscriber he needed to notify them of a change of address—to another high-security jail where he smokes Davidoffs, Cohibas, and (well ahead of the rest of the world) Trinidads.

Cigars have oiled the creative cogs of philosophers, artists, and composers for centuries. Charles Dickens, Albert Einstein, Sigmund Freud, Franz Liszt and Mark Twain were all enthusiastic cigar smokers.

In an odd sort of way, I feel I have walked in Papa Hemingway's historic footsteps, visiting his former home on Duval Street, Key West. Later, in Los Angeles, I was presented with an Arturo Fuente Hemingway Short Story, the smallest, noblest, and punchiest of a range of premium cigars, produced in the Dominican Republic by an exiled Cuban family. Then, in Paris, I talked cigars with Colin Field, head barman at the Ritz Hotel's Hemingway Bar. There, between noon and 9:30 p.m. on August 25, 1944, the author celebrated the Allied liberation of Paris by downing 51 gin martinis. I have also studied his photographs on the walls of El Floridita, another bar in Havana, where they still mix the rum and lime daiquiri that Hemingway drank when his home was in Cuba. At times, it felt as though he had only just left the room and might return at any moment.

For me, the mantle of Mr. Cigar goes to British showbiz impresario Lew Grade, now Lord Grade of Elstree. A struggling theatrical agent back in the 1940s, he first invested in a box of cigars to impress his clients, put them in his drawer, and promptly forgot about them.

**i**talian film crews on the classic Sixties spaghetti western kept Clint Eastwood's *Man With No Name* supplied with Toscani—the taste of Tuscany. The color and texture of sundried tomatoes, they smoke far better than they look.

# I lit up a Havana...and that was the day I was born.

LORD GRADE OF ELSTREE (right)

One day Lord Grade lit one up, "just to see what all the fuss was about," as he told *Cigar World* magazine. "And that was the day I was born." He has smoked seven Montecristo No. 2s every working day since, and proclaims, "there is still nothing better to put a guest at ease than to offer a Havana cigar."

Unquestionably the best-known cigar smoker of the 20th century was former British prime minister Sir Winston Churchill. He was voracious, getting through about ten a day. He would smoke in bed with a candle by his side to keep his cigar alight. Friends complained that he left a trail of cigar ash wherever he went.

Churchill favored a 7in. cigar, with a 47 ring gauge. He would smoke about half its length, the best of it in his opinion, and toss the remainder away. This Havana size is traditionally known in the Cuban factories as a *julieta*. However, in honor of a man who is reckoned to have smoked over 300,000 cigars during his life, many brands have renamed it the Churchill: the benchmark large cigar—the smoke of leadership.

I have always enjoyed the contrast between the image of Churchill—suit and homburg, smoking a cigar, every inch the Western statesman—and those of revolutionaries Fidel Castro and Che Guevara, in their green military fatigues: men-of-the-people dressed in the color of the land they fought for.

A lifelong asthma sufferer, Dr. Che Guevara nonetheless listed smoking as one of his top priorities. He went so far as to insist that every soldier include a supply of tobacco in his field-pack: "a companion to a solitary soldier," he once remarked. I don't know about his powder, but he certainly kept his cigar butts dry so that he could share his smokes with other revolutionaries in the field of war.

Guevara actually started smoking with a pipe, and he only switched to cigars in Cuba (favoring Montecristos, H.Upmanns, and Partagas) on learning that Cubans consider pipes to be a gringo pleasure. They called them *cachimba*, as in a Western six-shooter.

I don't drink, I do not smoke, I sleep a great deal. That is why I am in one-hundred percent form.

FIELD MARSHAL MONTGOMERY

i drink a great deal, I sleep little, and I smoke cigar after cigar. That is why I am in two-hundred percent form.

WINSTON CHURCHILL (left)

This page: Che Guevara
smoked a pipe in his native
Argentina, switching to the
cigar in Havana when his
revolutionary buddies pointed
out that pipes were for
Yankee gringos.
Left: Fidel Castro smoked
avidly for 44 years, until
his personal physician
insisted he quit.

# the power &
## the passion of Hollywood.

Cuba's president, Fidel Castro, was an avid smoker for 44 years, until his personal physician insisted that he quit. Castro may have gained some added pleasure from the fact that his former adversary, John F. Kennedy, suffered directly from the U.S.A. trade embargo with Cuba he himself instigated.

Shortly after the disastrous American-backed attempt to reinvade Cuba in 1961 (known as The Bay of Pigs), JFK summoned his cigar-smoking press secretary, Pierre Salinger, to the Oval Office. The President told him that he needed a lot of petit H.Upmanns. "How many?," asked Salinger. "At least 1,000. was the reply, "and quickly."

The next day White House officials were instructed to show Salinger directly to the President, the minute he showed up for work. And he had done well. Within 24 hours he had secured for his boss no fewer than 1,100 cigars.

"Good," declared JFK: enough of his favorite cigars to see him through the coming months. Whereupon he produced a document from a desk drawer and promptly signed it. That was the decree banning the importation of all Cuban products into the U.S.A. The President had taken care of his own needs, then put in place a trade embargo that continues to this day.

It is irrelevant that, for decades, cheap machine-made cigars for the working man and woman have rolled off production lines on both sides of the Atlantic. As far as cartoonists and lampooners are concerned, cigar smokers are overweight and overpaid. Otherwise they are characterized as gangsters—and perhaps with good reason.

Some years ago I worked in a bar on the wrong side of the tracks in southeast London. Each Christmas a crew of north London villains stopped by to pay their respects to a former associate who refused to inform on his accomplices during his years in prison. They were happy occasions, with many Havanas passed around to all and sundry. The only sour note, as I recall, was when one of their younger soldiers produced a Havana nearly twice the size of his boss's. For this insensitivity he was firmly requested to step outside with the offending object.

Gangsters were never so cruel to each other when New York tobacconist Nat Sherman was a boy. In those days, Big Apple gangsters used to drop by his father's store in the garment district.

"Bugsy Segal I remember, and some other very famous characters," says Nat, in the office of his 42nd Street store.

"The thing was, the store was neutral ground. You'd see these limousines pull up and men with bulges under their coats would get out. Guys were out killing each other on the docks, literally, and they'd come in and you'd hear them ask each other what they were smoking. 'Let me buy you one,' they would say. Cigars are a great leveler."

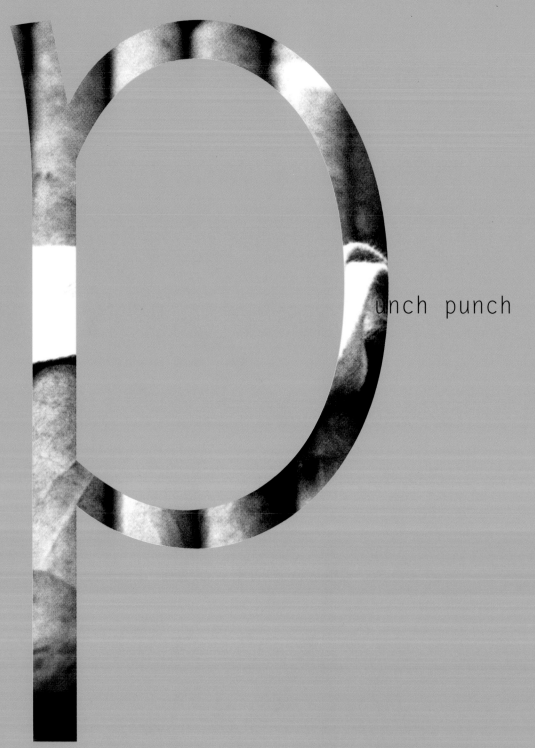

**p**unch punch

Right: Big hitter Arnold Schwarzenegger's
preferred cigar is Punch Punch, of course.

Left: Anthony Kiedis
of The Red Hot
Chili Peppers,
publicly outed for
sucking on a stogie
on the cover of
*Smoke* magazine.

This page:
His Latest Flame,
the King's secret
passion.

the cult of the cigarati is born when Madonna goes public smoking a cigar on U.S. network television.

Isabella Rossellini: suited and booted.

*Dialogue from an early scene in the Miramax film Smoke, written by Paul Auster. Augie (Harvey Keitel) is in his Brooklyn cigar store talking with customers Tommy and Jerry. In walks Paul Benjamin (William Hurt), a local novelist.*

**Paul:** Two tins of Schimmel-penninck... throw in a lighter while you're at it.

**Augie:** The boys and me were just having a philosophical discussion about women and cigars.

**Paul:** Well yeah, I suppose that goes back to Queen Elizabeth.

**Augie:** The Queen of England?

**Paul:** Not Elizabeth the Second, Elizabeth the First. D'you ever hear of Sir Walter Raleigh?

**Tommy:** Yeah sure, that's the guy who threw his cloak down over that puddle.

**Jerry:** I used to smoke Raleigh cigarettes, they came with a free gift coupon in every pack.

**Paul:** Well, Raleigh was the person who introduced tobacco into England and since he was a favorite of the queen's, Queen Bessie they used to call her, smoking caught on as a fashion. I'm sure old Bessie must have

shared a stogie or two with
Sir Walter. Once he made a bet
with her that he could measure
the weight of smoke.
Voice: You mean weigh smoke?
Paul: Exactly, weigh smoke.
Voice: You can't do that, it's
like weighing air.
Paul: I admit it's strange, it's
almost like weighing someone's
soul. Sir Walter was a clever guy
—he took an unsmoked cigar and
put it on a balance and weighed
it. Then he lit up, smoked the
cigar carefully, tapping the
ashes into the balance pan. When
he was finished he put the butt
into the pan along with the ashes
and weighed what was there and he
subtracted that number from the
original weight of the unsmoked
cigar. The difference was the
weight of the smoke.

t<sub>he best way</sub> to break a bad habit

is to replace it with a better one.

JACK NICHOLSON (right)

Pop stars who have confessed to smoking cigars include Madonna, who appeared on a national talk show with a cigar on the go; Janet Jackson, who smoked one on stage at an awards ceremony; sometime Spice Girl Geri Halliwell; and U2's Bono. All four members of The Red Hot Chili Peppers enjoy a cigar: "I know it's trendy," Chad Smith told *Smoke* magazine, "but I really enjoy them during certain activities—watching the Tyson fight, drinking, gambling."

Linda Evangelista is said to collect humidors, and Eva Herzigova, Kate Moss, and Elle MacPherson have all been photographed with cigars. According to a report in *Cigar Aficionado* magazine (August 1997), Claudia Schiffer puffed her way through an assortment of Cohiba robustos and Siglo 1Vs in addition to two Montecristos (Nos. 1 and 2), during a marathon, five-hour photographic session for a cover article. The supermodel's reward was being voted top cover girl by readers of the magazine.

*Cigar Aficionado* and *Smoke* magazines have been central to the cigar revival. Both are high-circulation, glossy titles, selling hundreds of thousands of copies.

Nothing denotes wealth and status quite as succinctly as a cigar. Aside from an appreciation of the good things in life and the ability to support expensive tastes, the person who wields it also displays a disregard for conventional public opinion and a willingness to take on a modicum of revolutionary chic.

The covers of these magazines (crammed as they are with all the appurtenances of what used to be known as the jet-set lifestyle—fast cars, designer clothes, glamorous accessories) are the perfect place to strike such a posture. And if, in the process, it helps to promote a film, book, record, or career, so much the better.

To paraphrase Jack Nicholson, who got his first taste of the weed while filming *The Last Detail* in 1973, the best way to break a bad habit is to replace it with a better one.

Should there ever be an award for the best supporting actor of the 20th century, the cigar will most certainly walk it. Cut... and light.

# burning desire

**W**ho are the modern cigar smokers, the new cigarati, the models and musicians, film-makers and new-wave bohemians fueling the cigar boom and filling cigar bars from London to Los Angeles?

My search takes me to London's Notting Hill. On a warm afternoon, two guys in T-shirts and combat fatigues take their pints of bitter and cigars outside a tiny Irish pub to enjoy the sunshine. The pulse of this shabby and chic corner of West London is always a beat or two slower than elsewhere in the capital, and the people who live and work here enjoy life at a civilized pace.

Traditionally British pubs are where drinkers smoke cigarettes and fretfully flick ash on the floor. But things are different at Tom Conran's Cow. Behind the bar, a glass case contains hand-rolled Cuban cigars; upstairs, the dining room is the setting for a unique London experience—cigar evenings, hosted by Tom Conran (pictured right).

"A lot of my friends are what I would call part-time cigar smokers," says Tom, leaning on the bar, "and the concept of an evening of fine food, wines, and good cigars appealed to them. In fact, they didn't need much convincing at all."

These are informal affairs, a far cry from the conventional cigar dinner, with their black ties and pomp. Here men and women, mostly in their 20s and 30s, share a passion for the Holy Smoke. Attending the inaugural dinner was Tom's father, Sir Terence Conran: restaurateur, style guru, publisher, and the man who has done more than most to galvanize New Britain's sense of good taste.

Elsewhere in London, cigar enthusiasts have new places to go—Monty's, The No. 1 Cigar Club, Havana, the cigar bar at Boisdales, and now Che: all of them contemporary settings where smokers can comfortably light up and relax.

Retailers are becoming less stuffy, too. TomTom is a shop and lounge, where people hang out and talk cigars. Owner Tom Assheton came up with the concept while soaking in the tub on board his houseboat, moored on the Thames in Chelsea.

"A lot of people are quitting cigarettes and moving over to cigars," says Tom, "and I wanted to offer them somewhere unlike the cigar shops their fathers went to... somewhere less formal, and frankly, funkier. They can have a juice or coffee, play some chess, and relax."

f or me, cigars
have changed the nature of
the whole smoking experience.

BRUCE SMITH, MUSICIAN (this page and left)

24A ▷                      25                  ▷  25A                26

18A ▷                      19                  ▷  19A                20

12A ▷                      13                  ▷  13A                14

26A    27

 27A    28

 20A    21

 21A    22

 14A    15

15A    16

# i
think it's the size I love.

JOSEPH ETTEDGUI, right, fashion designer and retailer

Previous page: Twins Mark and Michael Polish

Since arriving in London's Kensington from his native Morocco in the 1960s, designer and retailer Joseph Ettedgui has had a profound effect on the way fashionable London dresses and eats. He is an advocate of understated good taste, as evidenced by his choice of cigar: the Davidoff Special R, possibly the best-looking robusto of them all.

"I think it's the size I love," he tells me over a cup of coffee in one of his restaurants, Joe's Café. "The Special R is slightly thicker than others. Traditionally when they were thick like that, they would be very long too and that frightens people. A big cigar can be intimidating. Also, I can't have them so long with my height—I'm too short.

"I smoke, on average, at least two or three cigars a day.

Always when I am contemplating or when I am quiet at home, watching a video and there is nobody there at all. I always enjoy a cigar more when I am on my own than when I am with a group of people."

And does he think cigars are sexy? Are they the fashion accessory of the next millennium?

Yes, with reservations: "Depending on the mood of the photograph. When you think of the cigar you think of the tropics and Cuba and sunshine, and that is complimentary. If you wear all white and you have a shoot to do with a straw hat and there is a cigar—it seems very natural. But I don't like it when they use cigars in photographs in magazines just for the sake of it. I think a cigar is something that is quite real and beautiful and not just a prop."

Right: Australian waitress Martha Millan, at Cibar, New York.

my search moved on to New York, where Mark Grossich, one of the first aficionados to identify the new smoking trend, established Bars & Books, a dark, mischievously mysterious cigar lounge on Manhattan's Upper East Side. In his view, sophisticated urbanites in the 1990s have gladly made do with less, only if it happened to be the best.

"They may not be able to buy a Rolls Royce or a bespoke suit, but they can afford to buy a glass of the best single malt scotch and the best cigar, for 20 bucks," says Mark, whose customers include celebrated cigar smokers Mel Gibson and James Bond actor Pierce Brosnan. "It gives people pleasure to be able, with not a heck of a lot of money, to feel that they are enjoying something that is truly exceptional.

"People are socializing with style more than ever before. In Britain it's never really gone away, but in America we tend to go from one extreme to the other. One year it's casual, the next year it's formal. But I do think, now, that this whole cigar/cocktail lounge thing is here to stay." The evidence for this is in bars like Cibar, Club Macanudo, The Havana Tea Room, upstairs at Patroon, and Pravda.

A ten-dollar cab ride away, drummer Bruce Smith smokes cigars to help him concentrate in the studio. He acquired a taste for Havanas while working in London, initially with former girlfriend Neneh Cherry in Rip,

Rig and Panic and later with PiL. He played with the Sade band on their Sweetback project in 1997 and today he lives in the East Village and is in the throes of a Latin fusion project.

We meet, not in one of the many yuppie champagne and cigar bars in and around New York's financial district, but in a place called 7B, on the corner of Avenue B and Seventh Street.

It looks closed from the outside. We are still not convinced it is open as we shuffle through the glass-paneled door into the dark, unlit bar. A man drinks coffee from a white porcelain mug and the humidor, such as it is, comprises a beer glass stuffed with stogies from the Dominican Republic.

"I told you it wasn't chi chi," says Bruce. "Nothing fancy. Just a regular local bar for local people."

Bruce's is a fairly typical story. He likes smoking, but needed to quit cigarettes. "This guy gave me a cigar and said 'try this' and I thought wow, this is a whole other thing. What happened then... for a while, I probably smoked a few too many.

"But soon I found myself smoking less and enjoying it more. Now I go a day or two without smoking and not thinking about it. Instead of it being that kind of neurotic thing—dragging away on the old cigarette—it's an entirely new experience.

"Now, when I'm in the studio, it's something I can take a little time out for—and solve a problem with. It's subtle, and has changed my whole approach to smoking."

An old friend in Los Angeles emailed me about *Twin Falls Idaho*, the first full-length feature film by identical twin brothers Mark and Michael Polish (see pages 120-121). It is the story of Siamese twins, Blake (played by Mark) and Francis (Michael) Falls, and their struggle for acceptance in a hostile world.

On a windswept Santa Monica pier, beneath a fearful sky, Mark, who is 20 minutes older than his brother, explains the crucial scene. It takes place at a Halloween party, where everyone is in disguise and the twins can go undetected, without fear of the ridicule that follows them in public.

A magician comes up to them and levitates a cigar. He is doing it with his hands and they don't know how. Then the magician lifts the cigar up and places it into one of the twins' mouths. But the twins decide to go one better. "I inhale and Michael blows out the smoke...

"With Michael and I it is how much we depend on one another for so many things—while at the same time struggling for our own individuality. And yet we are stronger as one because, of course, we were meant to be one —and that is a big theme in the movie."

By now the word was out that a politically incorrect writer from the U.K. was in L.A., tracking down hip cigar smokers: There was a Colombian sculptor, a transvestite bar-man, a night-club manager, and a plumber! My instincts told me to contact Gabrielle—a "real rock chick with a passion for stogies," said an informer.

The following day, parked in a side street, in an immaculate 1957 Chevrolet, Gabrielle is somewhat modestly describing herself as a "sad old Goth"—pale complexion, dark lips, black hair, and tattoos. For her, big cigars are the last vice.

"I guess I took 'em up because I wanted to fit in," she says, fumigating the interior of the Chevy. I want to light up too, but I am afraid that if I do the smoke will be so intense I will lose sight of her. The former presenter of a children's television show, she was fired after an item on body-piercing was deemed unsuitable for infants. Now she manages rock-and-roll bands.

"I don't drink and I don't use drugs," she confides. "I cut drinking out years ago—my liver couldn't take it anymore—but I wanted to sit at the table and play poker with the boys, and smoke a cigar.

"My friends all think it's disgusting, especially because I only really like big cigars—Churchills, something decent—but it brings me a lot of peace.

"Often people will say to me 'What's a little girl like you doing smoking a big cigar?' I hear that all the time when I'm out. But I get the same thing about my tattoos. I'll go into a supermarket in Los Angeles and parents pull their kids close to them."

late that same evening I am huddled into the open-air smoking terrace of Goldfinger, a nightclub in the center of Hollywood. It is in the early days of a law forbidding smoking inside any public place—restaurant, bar, or club—and being law-abiding citizens, we are dutifully puffing away on a chilly terrace, while all the action is going on inside. The occasion is a birthday party for a girl called Kim, who is wearing a body-hugging, red, sequined dress. Kim runs a baroque-and-roll clothes store on Beverly Boulevard, and appears to be basketballer-tall, in her high heels and hair.

I am here to meet Kristine Lomis. She swapped her cigarettes for cigars and a small town in New Mexico for the Hollywood music scene.

"To change my life," she says, "I had to get out of one-horse towns and dead-end jobs. I dyed my hair, bought a box of cigarrillos, and began writing songs. Now, look at me, I'm a Rock Diva.

"Actually, I got the taste for cigars on the Greyhound bus. I was sitting at the back with a professor of philosophy. He told me about Cuba and the plantations and how the tobacco leaves are dried and how, when they are ready, they are rolled by hand. He said that such care gives it—the cigar—a spirituality. He called it 'chi' and this is what gives us strength. It wasn't the kind of story, or advice, you could ignore.

"People are afraid to smoke here. They even have smoking police—guys who go around clubs to make sure nobody is smoking. You know, I sing with a cigar on stage... not lit, just there, in my hand as a sort of prop, and someone reported that to the manager.

"There is no turning back though, I'm not kicking these, law or no law. This is me, and I like it that way."

"It's not so rare to see women smoking cigars now," says dancer Bunty Matthias, "with Madonna and Sharon Stone making it fashionable. But you still get comments. People seem to thinks it's funny, a woman with a big cigar."

I confess I raised an eyebrow, too, when I discovered Bunty's fondness for them, solely because Bunty is a ballet dancer. She has her own successful, London-based company, and an energetic lifestyle many

Cigar enthusiasts: Gabrielle page 129,
Bunty Matthias pages 130-131,
and Kristine Lomis pages 134-135.

would think incompatible with that of the leisurely cigar enthusiast.

"I like the look of cigars, and the whole production process. I prefer the 4½in., half-corona size Romeo y Julietas. Cohibas I find a bit too strong, too heavy.

"For me they are like brandy; I have to be in the mood. I love the 1920s and 1930s and cigars remind me of that period. They seem more elegant than a cigarette. Pulling one out feels novel and glamorous."

Cigars were never an option for Jake Scott, son of film director Ridley. They are as much a part of his family life as "camera - action." I met him in London, in a break from editing his first feature film, *Plunkett & Macleane*.

Jake has a long way to go to rival his uncle Tony Scott, another film director, who has a walk-in humidor in his California home and who gets through up to a dozen cigars a day. But a young man who takes two full humidors with him to the Czech Republic for an 11-week shoot is clearly not some fashion victim jumping on a bandwagon. Jake Scott loves his cigars.

Upstairs at London's Groucho Club, Jake explains: "My whole childhood has revolved around cigars. For my 16th birthday, one of my presents from my dad was a box of Montecristo No. 4s. My family always encouraged it as an alternative to cigarette smoking, but it can be very expensive.

"It took me a long time to feel comfortable about getting a cigar out in public though, even in somewhere like this. Over the years I have continuously smoked them, but only at home. Now I think it's different because there is such a fashion about them.

"I've searched around and tried different kinds. I like the Hoyo de Monterreys, but these Montecristo No.2's I still think are the best. The shape is a big part of it... that lovely pyramid shape, tapering at the end."

And exactly how many did he get through while filming?

"I gave a lot away," he confesses, with a wry smile. "It's a good way of getting the crew to like you, and give you that bit extra.

"Whenever we needed another hour of filming after a long day, it would be 'Here, have a cigar.' It never fails."

# Some people think wearing

the right pair of socks can affect the outcome

## of a game of soccer

Johnny Vaughan puts his faith in a

## Punch Punch.

Cigars can even have an effect on the outcome of a soccer game, or so British television presenter Johnny Vaughan likes to think. Johnny's passions are cowboy movies, old Mercedes-Benzes, and Punch Punches. These he stores in an 18th-century humidor, a present from his girlfriend. To light them he employs another treasured gift—a glass oil lamp.

"It's a kind of cigar light," says Johnny with typical enthusiasm. "You get your wick burning nicely. Sometimes I really have had cigars soured by the taste of sulfur on the match, or off a candle or a lighter. But there is something about lighting your cigar with a strip of cedar from the actual cigar box. No aftertaste and you really feel it's the complete Cuban experience."

His other passion is soccer. Each Saturday he and his friends join forces to smoke their team, Chelsea, to victory.

"Three Punch Punches, a couple of H.Upmanns and maybe a Cohiba or two—all belching it out. The stewards really don't like it and we've had a few complaints. I wait until the game is a few minutes in, and I think the team needs a little bit of a lift. The problem is if we've scored a few goals while the cigar has been lit, I have to keep it going.

"You really can delude yourself that your cigar is affecting what is happening on the field of play. Some people think a pair of socks can influence the outcome—for me, it's a cigar."

Back in Notting Hill, Tom Conran has painstakingly removed the cap of the Montecristo No.2 I have given him.

"Mmm," he intones, striking a match and savoring the aroma of charred tobacco. "These Cuban cigars have all been hand-rolled, and you have the sensation that somebody has nurtured the thing... taken time and considerable care."

He looks up. "Don't you think they have created a marvel?" Of that, I say, I am quite certain.

a young film director who takes two full humidors with him to the Czech Republic for an 11-week shoot is clearly not some fashion victim jumping on a bandwagon. Jake Scott, pictured right, simply loves cigars.

the right stuff

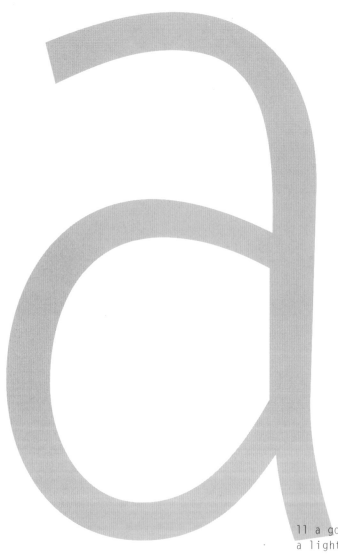

ll a good cigar really needs is a light. There is, nonetheless something compelling about cigar accessories. Crafted with as much care and precision as the smokes themselves, these highly cherished items—cutters, lighters, cases, and humidors— are intimately associated with moments of true pleasure.

Right: Alfred Dunhill solid silver cigar scissors: the surgical way to slice a stogie.

Cigar scissors.

bill amberg, a modern aesthete, photographed with his 21st-century humidor.

# at rest in a humidor

cigars can be convinced that they remain in the tropics.

To ensure their optimum condition, cigars should be stored at temperatures between 61°F and 70°F, at a relative humidity of 65 to 70 percent. Even if you are at the North Pole, your cigars will be happier if you can convince them that they, at least, remain in the tropics—Cuba's Pinar del Rio, if at all possible.

Hence the need for a humidor, a solid wooden box, often made of walnut or mahogany and usually lined with cedar. They are fitted with humidifying units to maintain the correct levels of moisture and temperature inside. These units vary, although a common one, like that in my black, lacquered Davidoff humidor, is an encased carbon "sponge." This is clamped to the lid and filled up with water every few weeks. The lid of a humidor should be heavy and should close firmly, but not too tightly, as a good circulation of air is essential for the cigars to remain "fresh."

Cigars can be kept for years like this and the only real danger, then, is "cigar beetles." If the cigars become too damp—regulating how much water to use is a matter of trial and error—these tiny pests will bore holes in the contents, leaving behind telltale traces of dust. If they do strike, don't throw away your entire stock, but try transferring the cigars to a refrigerator for a couple of days. This should kill the beetles. Before you return the cigars to the humidor wipe down the cedar lining with a clean, damp cloth.

Good humidors are not cheap: $1,200 to $1,600 to start. Plexiglas ones are cheaper, while really vulgar ones can cost several times that amount. In the long run it pays to have something of quality.

If your habit takes off and you find you do not have enough room for your burgeoning stock, ask your cigar merchant about storage facilities. These are also the people to talk to if your cigars have dried out. The patience and skills of a good supplier should be able to breathe new life back into them in time.

Most humidors serve to reinforce the gentleman's club notion of cigars. However, for food entrepreneur Oliver Peyton's latest London restaurant, Mash, designer Bill Amberg threw out all preconceived ideas and devised a humidor fit for the 21st century.

"I designed the humidor with an architect called Andrew Martin, and rather than worry about what a humidor should look like, we started from scratch, while keeping the principal elements of cedar lining and humidification."

The result is a cylindrical red leather shell which contains a cedar lining and a nickel-plated shelf, for around 100 cigars. Other versions will follow in dark brown crocodile tan, hand-stitched English bridle, and Havana leathers.

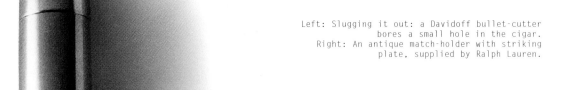

I once knew a Hungarian poet in Paris who grew the thumbnail of his right hand to around half-an-inch in length and honed the outer edge with a sandpaper file. I remember watching him slip the nail under the cap of his cigar and slowly work it around it, opening the end without loosening the wrapper.

Since then, I have met many people (although without such a precision appendage), designer Joseph Ettedgui among them, who favor this method of opening the capped end of their cigar. Cigars, they say, are natural, organic things, and it is simply too cold-blooded to slice the end off with a steel blade.

Nevertheless, blades remain the single most popular method of "releasing" a cigar.

The cheapest and most common blade is a simple guillotine in a small plastic holder, which tobacconists usually throw in with a selection of cigars. There are also double-bladed, two-finger cutters; hefty V-shaped cutters designed to remove an eye-shaped wedge; and bullet-cutters employing the same principle as the potato gun, which I had as a boy: a short, sharp-edged tube is bored into the cap, which leaves behind a small cavity when extracted. Knives, tabletop guillotines, and special cigar scissors with beveled edges are often stored in lids of humidors.

Some of the most elegant are circular cutters, designed to be attached to a keyring. Davidoff, Dupont, and Dunhill make them, at prices from about $100.

In the Tabac George V in Paris, I came across a gadget that looked like a miniature corkscrew, designed to be inserted into the shoulder (the closed head or cap) of the cigar several times, according to how much draw is required.

Whichever method you use, it is important to have a steady hand. Cut too far and you risk breaking the fragile connection between cap and binder and the cigar will unravel in your mouth. Too shallow and you may crunch the end together, again restricting the flow of smoke: natural tobacco oils could be funneled into a small part of the end, which would become sticky and taste bitter.

Cuban tobacco farmers, cowboys, and U.S. truckers bite the ends off their cigars. Some people consider this clumsy, not to say risky, particularly when they have paid the equivalent of a decent bottle of Burgundy for a single cigar and would rather smoke it than eat it.

Ultimately, like everything to do with cigars, take care and do it right. After all, have you anything better to do with your time?

For the wrist that speaks for itself:
"Be A Man—Smoke Cigars" cufflinks
from Brooks Brothers, New York.

there are
desirable cigar-
themed sweatshirts,
ties, umbrellas,
barbecues and golf-
caddy holders, but
*Up In Smoke* would
rather invest in a
good cigar than any
of these. We do,
however, make a
notable exception
for cigar cufflinks;
discretion being
the greater part of
cigarati style.

When a single cigar
can cost as much as a
good bottle of wine, it
is essential to keep
one's stock under lock
and key. Customers of
Patroon in New York
(see Clubbing) are
presented with this
hefty, bronze padlock to
secure their stogies.

<sup></sup>

tiffany cigar cutters.

Once your cigar is cut, light up. Any match could do the job, but you should be careful to avoid those that are waxed or have a high sulfur content, as these will be detrimental to the taste. Gasoline lighters should be avoided for the same reason.

Butane gas lighters are the best. The flame burns evenly and is odorless. Some even have integrated guillotines or cigar punches. Dupont makes a handsome double flame butane lighter in silver or gold, and black lacquer.

The fashion now, particularly among the active set, is for jet lighters: high-tech, high-pressure butane gas guns with a concentrated blue flame you could weld steel with. Useful, too, should you lose the key to the humidor.

Ashtrays bearing the logos and names of leading cigar brands are very collectible. At the cigar dinner in Havana there was a frantic dash for the first shipment of large white ashtrays with the name Trinidad.

g ucci ashtray.

# how cigars • breed new passions

International style guru and restaurateur Sir Terence Conran is a creature of some routine when it comes to smoking cigars.

"I enjoy four a day," he says, "and the first is started when I come down to the office in the morning. Someone brings me a cup of excellent coffee, and the first Havana is lit. I love the aroma, the sensation. Smoking is a serious business.

"One of the things I love is the paraphernalia that surrounds cigars. Everything seems very considered and beautifully simple: humidors; big, generous ashtrays; the slivers of cedar that line a good box of Havanas, and which can be used to light your cigar; the yellow ribbon that binds my Hoyo de Monterrey No.2s into a bundle in their box."

Needing an ashtray befitting his precious Hoyos, Sir Terence turned to Swiss sculptor Christiane Golinelli. She has lived and worked in New York for the past five years and has several of her pieces on display at Quaglinos, one of Sir Terence's London restaurants.

"He wanted something nice to rest a gently smoldering cigar on. He made it sound so poetic," says Christiane.

"I decided to base it on a shape that I am exploring in all my work—the dome. For me it's an obsessive visual theme, endlessly reshaped. There is a cradle for the cigar to rest on as it burns and a cup which comes away for the ash." Both components are fashioned in clay, glazed with terra sigillata, and fired at 1,800°F. 'Something to add pleasure to the cigar ceremony," she says.

A problem shared by all cigar enthusiasts is how physically to transport a small supply of cigars without damaging them. Hefty ones, like Churchills and robustos, may look as tough as old boots, but the truth is they are gentle giants: one false move can unravel months or years of painstaking work.

For most, the solution is an expandable leather case, usually made to hold two, three, or four cigars, with a top that slides up and down to accommodate a variety of lengths. The really strong ones have a stainless-steel core.

In the United States a minor industry produces cigar cases for every occasion: for the traveler, with compartments for travel documents and electronic personal organizers; for golfers, that clip onto a caddy and contain golf tees and score sheets in addition to a lighter and cigars. And then there is my favorite, the Nat Sherman Stadium Flask. The ultimate Big Apple accessory: a pewter hip flask and a secret compartment, big enough for a brace of coronas.

However ingenious, they all play havoc with the cut of a jacket.

Christiane Gollinelli's
resting place:
fit for a style guru.

"every cigar smoker should have a couple of tubos cigars like these, with screw-top, aluminum tubes, in their collection," explains Edward Sahakian of Davidoff, London, picking out a Bolivar No. 1. "They have a thin cedar lining and when you have smoked the cigar you can always use it again for others. No need for anything fancy.

"However, this is my daytime smoke," he says with a smile, proffering the small Davidoff Ambassadrice. "So I had something made that looks almost like a fountain pen that my cigar fits into." The initials E.S. are engraved on the side (left).

"Maybe I am smoking and I am called to a plane or I want to go into a shop—I slide my cigar into it and put it into my pocket and it remains there until I have the opportunity to continue smoking. This is my favorite piece of paraphernalia and I always carry it when I travel."

Fozzie Bear chews on a dog stogie supplied by Celebrity Pets in the U.S.A. Blends include Mutt Donna and Arnold Schnauzernegger. Fozzie Bear, on her home turf in London's Regent's Park, favors the fuller flavor of a Groucho Barks and, being by nature a rebellious Airedale terrier, keeps her cigar band on to the last.

bolivar

r omeo

el rey del mundo

la gloria cubana

hoyo de monterrey

cohiba

trinidad

vegas robaina

the knowledge

y **j**ulieta

A little knowledge goes a long way when choosing a cigar. Select the wrong one at the outset and you could end up kicking what ought to be an enjoyable habit, even before it has begun.

Leaving aside, for the moment, characteristics such as flavor and size, cigars are sold in a variety of strengths—from the milder blends, perfect for beginners or as a morning smoke, all the way through to rich, full-flavored stogies, suitable only for the experienced enthusiast—and even then, only after a rich meal.

This is the era of designer labels and some of the universally known brands are clearly too tempting for the uninitiated. I have met many occasional smokers—birthdays, Christmas, and New Year—who light up expensive, full-strength Havanas (often large prestige cigars from Bolivar or Cohiba) only to spend the rest of the day staring at the inside of a toilet. Their lesson: that the right cigar in the wrong hands can be a cruel and miserable experience.

# Often as not the narrower the ring gauge the hotter and spicier the cigar will burn.

As a basic rule of thumb, hand-rolled Cuban cigars are fuller flavored than those from the Dominican Republic, Honduras, Nicaragua, or elsewhere, which tend, for the most part, to be lighter. The traditional Cuban is rich and spicy whereas those from other Caribbean countries, selling in large numbers in the U. S. A., are far milder.

This is not to say that all Cubans are out of bounds for the novice. H.Upmann and Rafael Gonzalez are classic Cuban brands with extensive ranges any beginner can enjoy, confident that they are smoking something reputable and of real quality.

Edward S. Sahakian, at the Davidoff shop in London's St. James's, is frequently asked for advice.

"If you are a beginner and you want to smoke a cigar," he says surveying the contents of his walk-in humidor. "I would say try either a mild Dominican cigar, or something mild from the Havana range. I would take you straight to an H.Upmann, or otherwise an El Rey del Mundo. In fact, I have started more people on the H.Upmann Petit than any

other. A small cigar, 4½in. long and quite slim, it will last you at least half an hour. It is mild and a good starting point.

"From there on I would guide a beginner into trying a Montecristo. They are fuller, but fine after a nice meal, with a glass of brandy or port; or a Romeo y Julieta Exhibition No.3. It's a bit fatter, and 5½in. long, certainly full bodied and full of flavor, but gain, not very strong."

It is worth remembering that all the cigars in a range, produced by the same brand, will have the same flavor, or thereabouts. However, these are all individually hand-rolled cigars, incorporating wholly natural products. Minor variations in the color and burning qualities are bound to occur. The real differences within a brand, then, are to be found in the length, the girth (called a ring gauge and measured in 64ths of an inch) and the shape. All affect the amount of smoke drawn into the mouth, thereby altering the intensity of what is otherwise a "brand-constant" flavor.

Note, too, that just because a cigar is long and narrow it is not necessarily any milder, or lighter, than something twice its size. As often as not the narrower the ring gauge the ...

Appearance is very important, and this is an area where many Cuban brands are literally coming unstuck. You may be offered blotchy cigars, some that are split and frayed at the ends, and others where the fine wrapper leaf is coming away. Good retailers are only too aware of quality-control problems and they will usually suggest you sift through a box until you find one you like the look of. In a shop in Havana, I watched a pair of young American aficionados reject a dozen boxes of Punch Punch before they were satisfied.

Do not be too concerned about color, though. The outer wrapper leaf of Cuban cigars provides less than ten percent of the overall taste and is there for aesthetics and not flavor. It is what is inside and how it is put together that counts.

Search for a cigar with a smooth, even surface, without too many visible veins in the wrapper leaf. It should have a light iridescent patina and pleasant aroma. And finally, if it has been stored correctly, and in the right conditions, it should be ever so slightly soft in the center. Give it a little squeeze—not too much, though. If it is hard, or brittle, it will burn unevenly. And by the way, only a fool puts a cigar to his or her ear and listens to it.

As for size, that's up to you. I personally prefer a big smoke; long panatelas with narrow ring gauges and tubby corona grandes and Churchills. I am what may be described as vertically challenged, and there is a school of thought that says you should only smoke a cigar that reflects your size.

"Absolute rubbish," says Edward S. Sahakian, defiantly. "A cigar is there to give you pleasure. You should choose and smoke any one that you like. The only thing you buy in proportion to your size is your suit and shirt."

The sequence in which you smoke your cigars is important, though. I know a man who starts the day with a 7in. Churchill, smoking ever smaller cigars throughout the day and finishing with a half corona before bed. This is because he wants to be wide awake when he smokes his biggest and best cigars, and he is normally too drunk to care when he turns in.

That is far from normal practice. The received wisdom is to start small and light, and build up in size and strength as you go through the day: logical really. You will not extract much flavor from a Davidoff Ambassadrice if you have just finished a full-strength Cohiba Robusto. By the same token you will not derive much pleasure from a meal if you have first neutralized your tastebuds with a Bolivar corona gigante.

The trick is to take your time (I can make a cigar last all night), smoke in stages, and only after a meal, however light. Any cigar smoked on an empty stomach can prove to be fatal, and the objective, after all, is pleasure, not pain.

## 50 TOP SMOKES

Not necessarily the greatest cigars in the world, nor the most popular, but the cigars recommended to me during research for *Cigar Cool*. Cigar reviewers tend to use the culinary metaphors favored by wine tasters, but after a while, they tend to sound alike. Instead, I have chosen to use the cigar industry's own five-point strength-grading scale: light, light to medium, medium, medium to full, and full.

## QUINTERO
### purito

4 ¼ x 29 Cuba

*Behind-the-ear-sized, anytime cigar whose chocolate, bark-like exterior belies a soothing, mellow smoke.*

## H.UPMANN
### petit upmann

4 ½ x 31 Cuba

*Creamy and smooth; several retailers recommend this as the perfect beginners' or morning cigar. The politically incorrect even suggest it as "one for the ladies."*

## RAFAEL GONZALEZ
### tres petit lonsdale

4 ½ x 40 Cuba

*I was not prepared for the earthy, almost farmyard flavors of this complex and highly respected cigar, nor for the concentration required to keep it alight.*

## H.UPMANN
### petit corona

5 ½ x 42 Cuba

*Light, but with bite. Tightly rolled in an appealing greenish/ brown wrapper, with a firm draw, and surprisingly rich for one so mild.*

## MACANUDO
### vintage no.III

5 ½ x 43 Jamaica

*Once a firm favorite in the U.K. and today the best-selling brand in the U.S.A. A smooth, creamy, everyday smoke.*

## CASA BLANCA
### de luxe

6 x 50 Dominican Republic

*A lamb in wolf's clothing. Not the bruiser the slightly oily Mexican oscuro wrapper suggests. Instead, a sweet daytime smoke with an attractive, brilliant white ash.*

## NAT SHERMAN
### tribeca

6 x 31 Dominican Republic

*One of the Manhattan range, dressed in a woody Mexican wrapper, and the ideal alternative to a morning cup of coffee.*

## ROYAL JAMAICA
### corona grande

6 ½ x 42 Dominican Republic

*Traditionally a mild brand. In this "maduro" size, with a Brazilian wrapper, it has attack and real depth.*

### DAVIDOFF
### 3000

7 x 33 Dominican Republic

*Exquisitely tailored in claro Connecticut wrapper, and an object lesson in rolling perfection. Cool, almost menthol on the draw, with a light, nutty aftertaste.*

### SANCHO PANZA
### corona gigante

7 x 47 Cuba

*Perfect for the beginner looking to impress. It is chunky in appearance yet cool, satisfying, and undemanding.*

### MOORE & BODE
### no.10

7 ½ x 50 U.S.A.

*Very impressive, with a mottled claro wrapper, this slightly salty Miami blend, in the double corona size, is subtly satisfying.*

### EL REY DEL MUNDO
### tres petit corona

4 ½ x 40 Cuba

*Wonderfully smooth, instantly appealing, superbly presented. Long live the self-anointed "king."*

### DAVIDOFF
### special R

4 ⅞ x 50 Dominican Republic

*An iridescent sheen and tasteful white band make this the prettiest of all the robustos. An object lesson in perfection of quality and taste.*

### EL REY DEL MUNDO
### choix supreme

5 x 48 Cuba

*Simon Chase, of U.K. cigar importers Hunters & Frankau, suggested this slightly dry and salty Havana as an ideal pre-dinner, cocktail accompaniment. Right again.*

### SANTA DAMIANA
### seleccion no.500

5 x 50 Dominican Republic

*The robusto size of a top-quality range, reintroduced during the mid-90s, with a fuller flavor, and aimed at European smokers with their penchant for spicy Havanas. An unqualified success.*

### PAUL GARMIRIAN
### robusto

5 x 50 Dominican Republic

*This feels fabulous: tightly rolled and sturdy. Impeccably cut and an excellent, aromatic daytime smoke that really develops and evolves with time.*

### PAUL GARMIRIAN
### belicoso

6 ½ x 52 Dominican Republic

*A case of a cigar connoisseur and author putting his own stogies where his mouth is. His achievement? A top-quality Dominican that smokes like a Cuban. Very tasty.*

## ARTURO FUENTE
### reserva no.1

6 ⁵/₈ x 44 Dominican Republic

*One of the limited edition Opus X range, and rarer than hens' teeth. A complex, engaging smoke with an oily, almost antique wrapper, containing a symphony of sweet spices.*

## JOYO DE NICARAGUA
### no.10

6 ½ x 43 Nicaragua

*Strikingly different and yet extremely enjoyable. A firm, greeny/claro wrapper and a lingering, dry, nutty taste on the palate.*

## ARTURO FUENTE
### lonsdale

6 ½ x 42 Dominican Republic

*All Fuentes feel solid, like sticks of wood, with a sleek, glossy sheen. Few, however, are as neutral and balanced as this.*

## MOORE & BODE
### full brass

7 ¹/₄ x 64 U.S.A.

*If you can adjust to having something the size of an Olympic torch in your mouth. This is an incredibly smooth cigar that never fails to raise eyebrows and provoke comment, steadily building as it glows.*

## COHIBA
### siglo I

4 x 40 Cuba

*Small in stature but not in strength. When time is tight, this refined anniversary blend provides a hearty blast of pure Havana.*

## HOME ROLLED PUROS
### panetela

5 x 36 Cuba

*There is not an adult Cuban alive who cannot roll a cigar. The quality of farm-rolled cigars varies enormously, but they are always delicious. Ask around.*

## HOYO DE MONTERREY
### epicure no.2

4 ⁷/₈ x 50 Cuba

*Topping a Cigar Aficionado blind tasting, with 92 out of a maximum 100 points. What a fabulous cigar, too-richly aromatic, with the undeniable taste of coffee and nutmeg. Everyone's favorite robusto.*

## ROMEO Y JULIETA
### exhibicion no.4

5 x 48 Cuba

*One to aspire to. A demanding, connoisseur's cigar that should not even be considered until after a hearty meal, and only then when it can be given your undivided attention.*

## PUNCH
### punch punch

5 ⁵/₈ x 46 Cuba

*I love this cigar, erratic quality control notwithstanding. A balanced, spicy, robust, value-for-money, compelling smoke for any occasion.*

## EL REY DEL MUNDO
### flor de llaneza

6 ½ x 54 Honduras

*Lew Rothman, of the J.R. discount cigar empire, declared this the best in his store. When you consider his Whippany, New Jersey outlet is bigger than most aircraft hangars, that is some claim!*

## LA GLORIA CUBANA
### medaille d'or 4

6 x 32 Cuba

*Outwardly a bit patchy, but firmly packed and with an increasingly insistent flavor.*

## COHIBA
### siglo V

6 ¹¹/₁₆ x 43 Cuba

*Tall, not too dark, and very handsome. Mellow and aromatic, medium-flavored, and with a palate-friendly, evanescent sweetness. Very classy.*

## VEGAS ROBAINA
### familiar 42

5 ⁷/₁₂ x 42 Cuba

*Bearing the name of Cuba's most celebrated tobacco grower. A class act: a deceptively rustic appearance, bursting with dark chocolate and oozing sophistication.*

## LA GLORIA CUBANA
### taino

7 x 47 Cuba

*Genuinely versatile. Without the seductive sheen of more prestigious Churchills, it succeeds with that winning combination of medium strength and full flavor.*

## ROMEO Y JULIETA
### churchill

7 x 47 Cuba

*Not entirely evocative of the Bulldog Breed, being the light side of medium, but a substantial, stately, and consistently cool smoke.*

## HOYO DE MONTERREY
### double corona

7 ⁵/₈ x 49 Cuba

*Pure refinement and unsurpassed smoking pleasure. Best enjoyed in total isolation, wherein nothing can detract from the soft, mildly spiced flavors and the lingering, fragrant aftertaste.*

## CUABA
### generoso

5 ³/₁₆ x 42 Cuba

*The world's first retro cigar, launched in 1996 and intended to appeal to British traditionalists who hanker for something a bit different. Provides a pleasant, aromatic smoke, not unlike a pipe.*

## COHIBA
### robusto

4 ⅞ x 50 Cuba

*Deserving every bit of praise heaped upon it. A tight, shiny, oily wrapper, an effortless draw, and bags of spice. The benchmark medium-to-full robusto.*

### MONTECRISTO
### No.2

6 ⅛ x 52 Cuba

*The brand's distinctive spiciness is intensified by the pyramid shape. One of the great cigars, if you can find one that is not falling apart.*

### HOYO DE MONTERREY
### le hoyo des dieux

6 1/12 x 42 Cuba

*The French magazine L'Amateur de Cigare rated this the best of all the Hoyos. Cut to perfection, complex, aromatic—leather and chocolate—and thoroughly absorbing. Heavenly indeed!*

### NAT SHERMAN
### algonquin

6 ¾ x 43 Dominican Republic

*A terrific, full-flavored fruity cigar that continues to develop and satisfy during the 90 minutes or so it is alight.*

### MONTECRISTO
### especial no.1

7 9/16 x 38 Cuba

*A box of these was my constant companion in Cuba. The shape to supersede the robusto perhaps— the same size as a Cohiba lancero. Perfectly weighted, with a warm, steady burn.*

### COHIBA
### esplendido

7 x 47 Cuba

*Bags of medium-flavor character. As unputdownable as a favorite book. Clear your diary before lighting up and give it the attention it deserves.*

### DON RAMOS
### no.11

6 ¾ x 47 Honduras

*Without the soft, aromatic aftertaste of the best Cubans, its greeny/claro wrapper is at variance with the tawny filler. An uncomplicated, pleasant smoke, nonetheless.*

### MONTECRISTO
### 'a'

9 ¼ x 47 Cuba

*The flagship cigar of Cuba's most popular brand. A spectacular statement of smoking defiance. Tiers of dark, spicy flavors; it takes three hands just to light it and a full evening to enjoy.*

### PARTAGAS
### shorts

4 ⅓ x 42 Cuba

*Breaktime-size with a distinctive, deep, full flavor. Try having an unpleasant thought while you're smoking it—it isn't easy. An aide to pleasant contemplation.*

### BOLIVAR
### petit corona

5 1/12 x 42 Cuba

*With a sleek, iridescent wrapper, this baby Bolivar punches above its weight.*

## PARTAGAS
## serie D no.4

4 ⁷/₈ x 50 Cuba

*Powerful, rich, totally absorbing, like stuffing your mouth with Christmas cake and vintage port. Leaves your tastebuds reeling for hours.*

## SAINT LUIS REY
## regio

5 x 48 Cuba

*Outstanding. An oily, iridescent wrapper, a slow, effortless, even burn, a delicate sweetness on the palate, and, actually, much milder than its reputation leads us to believe.*

## PARTAGAS
## corona

5 ⁵/₁₂ x 42 Cuba

*The classic Havana. Dark and brooding, light on the draw, billowing smoke, with a peppery, almost sour aftertaste. Recommended for advanced enthusiasts only, but richly rewarding for those who dare.*

## MONOPOLI DI STATO
## toscani

6 x 36 Italy

*There is something darkly wicked about this slow burner from Tuscany. Chewed by Clint Eastwood in the 60s "Dollar" films, it needs to be cut in half, prior to lighting, and accompanied by tequila or grappa.*

## TRINIDAD
## fundador

7 ½ x 40 Cuba

*Darkly flavorsome, yet soft and seductive on the palate. Involves you from the second you light up. Not so much "new kid on the block" as impeccably prepared debutante.*

## BOLIVAR
## corona gigante

7 x 47 Cuba

*Infinitely better in larger sizes, although not for the beginner, these noble smokes assault the senses from the moment they touch the lips. Best to indulge after a full meal, off-set with intoxicating liquor.*

# How to spot a fake

It's not hard to sucker tourists, particularly in the Caribbean, who may not know how to identify a genuine cigar. As the worldwide popularity of premium hand-rolled cigars continues to grow, what used to be a small cottage industry in counterfeits has grown into a major criminal activity.

Fakes are made from unblended, stolen bits of broken leaves. In the Dominican Republic there is not even an attempt to appear genuine. I was offered a box of Cohibas that might have been rolled by a chimpanzee in boxing gloves. The labels and cigars were all different sizes. Slicing the end off one of the contents, whatever they were (not tobacco as we know it), it came apart like a ball of string.

To outwit the counterfeiters and reassure consumers, genuine Cuban cigars carry three hallmarks burnt into the underside of each box. One reads Habano S.A., the official Cuban cigar export agency; another *hecho en Cuba*—made in Cuba—and the third, *totalmente a mano*—totally by hand. A fourth safeguard is a 4½ in. by 7½ in. green and white government wraparound seal. Since 1994, boxes also carry a red and yellow Habanos chevron in the top right-hand corner.

Sadly, all of these methods are available to counterfeiters, who steal them from the factories. This has led some international importers to introduce their own security devices, such as the EMS (English Market Selection) stamp in the U.K.

# robusto

## How to deal with ash

Cigar bands, those intricately embellished paper rings bearing the brand name and logo, were created during the 18th century, initially, so the story goes, for Russian women smokers who did not want to taint their white evening gloves with tobacco stains and smells. But what was a sensible solution 200 years ago is today a matter that openly divides the cigar-smoking community: should the band remain on the cigar during smoking, or should it be removed?

The general consensus comes down heavily in favor of the latter, and is endorsed by author G. Gabrera Infante in his witty and perceptive account of cigars, *Holy Smoke*. "The band, though placed around the cigar last," he writes, "must always come off first, no matter what bogus connoisseurs might tell you."

The reasoning is that smoking with the band on is vulgar and horribly *nouveau riche*. By wearing your prestige label you intimidate someone with a cheaper or less prestigious smoke.

To be honest, I prefer to keep the band on because I think it lends character. By the same token I would never attempt to remove the label from a bottle of wine.

If, however, you are a stickler for protocol, do not attempt to tear the band off an unlit cigar, lest you rip the wrapper. Wait until the cigar is lit and has reached what the late Zino Davidoff described as its *temperature de croisière*—cruising temperature—and the gum holding the band together has softened.

More controversy surrounds the accumulation of ash, as though the longer the ash the better the smoke. I have seen Wall Street traders holding their stogies aloft, as though breathing through a snorkel, in an attempt to hold on to a tower of ash.

Certainly a firm, even ash that maintains its shape for an inch or more is a sign of a well-rolled cigar. Yet there is another argument: that too much ash impedes the flow of air, heats up the cigar, and adversely affects the process of smoking.

Best simply to allow the ash to fall off naturally, in its own good time, and stop worrying about matters of such little consequence.

Robusto rules! Modern smokers like girth without length. This, some say, is because they don't care for ostentatious cigars; others that they are simply too busy to smoke a corona. Thus, the defining shape of the turn of the century is—the robusto. Traditionally around 5in. long with a 48-50 ring gauge, it's a pocket-rocket and a sign of the times.

# Cape & Volute: a woman's choice

Increasing numbers of female cigarati in Paris are turning to a women's only club, Cape et Volute. The club meets once a month for a meal and two cigars, and members are drawn from all walks of life, their ages ranging from 30 to 60.

Its president is Valerie Kerever: "For years I never saw women smoking cigars," she says, "and suddenly there are so many; all the French feminist magazines are writing about them.

"Women come to us because we are genuinely interested in cigars, good food and good wine. They take these things very seriously, and are very knowledgeable."

Seated in Le Fumoir, a popular smoking lounge close to the Louvre in central Paris, Valerie told me about her career in public relations with a champagne and wine company, and how her introduction to cigars was a Punch Punch, given to her by the chef at a promotions dinner.

"Nowadays I like a Sancho Panza Non Plus, essentially a petit corona. It is not too strong, but the perfumes are woody and it burns evenly. The Non Plus is a little, elegant cigar which suits at such times. After an evening meal I treat myself to something more imposing, but still I don't want something too overbearing. The Juan Lopez Seleccion No.1, a corona gorda, is also rather light, but very aromatic. There are subtle flavors on the palate, and an oiliness. I would say that it is a glutton's cigar, or rather, a gourmet's cigar that is big but never over-filling..."

(For details of Cape et Volute and Le Fumoir see Clubbing on page 179.)

# the Ritz, Paris:
## top five cigars & cocktails

At the Hemingway Bar at the Ritz Hotel, Paris, head barman Colin Field prides himself on matching the person to the cocktail ("All I need to know is how you feel") and the cocktail to the cigar. These are his top five matches made in heaven.

### 1. H.Upmann Sir Winston.
(also called a Monarcas). Spicy, orange peel, lemon, ginger, coffee and cream, going into pepper and chocolate.

With it a Ponsonby—one third cognac, two-thirds port over ice. Have it as an aperitif, an early-evening lift. Many less hardened drinkers may prefer it at the end of the evening.

### 2. Sancho Panza Belicosos.
This is a beautiful cigar, with chocolate going into pepper and caramels. Marvellous with a 15-year-old Abelour single malt, with a drop of Grand Marnier. On its own the whiskey has a slightly orange smell and if you enhance it with the liqueur you have the classic culinary combination of chocolate and oranges that awakens the palate rather than sends it to sleep.

### 3. Romeo y Julieta Cazadores.
five to ten years old. A very powerful cigar that begins with pepper, then moves into coffee and something the French describe as "animal smells," which basically means horse manure. With this the Mk ll Landsburg. Two-thirds whiskey and one-third green Chartreuse and a few drops of fresh ginger steeped in vodka. A powerful end of the evening, a knock-you-for-six cocktail.

### 4. Partagas Londsdale, Cabinet Selection 50.
An extremely rare cigar. In an old-fashioned glass, pour one-tenth Angostura bitters and nine-tenths cognac, and lots of ice. This cocktail has the feeling of a Manhattan, but ice gives the cognac a slightly spicy edge which complements the spiciness of the Londsdale superbly.

### 5. Romeo y Julieta Cedros No.3.
A cheap cigar, and just the sort to take on country walks, with cedar wood protection so it won't get damaged in your pocket. The finest accompaniment is the dry, smokey, dark Caol Ila whiskey. Keep some in a hip flask, and with the Cedros you have the perfect pairing.

# the cigar dinner

To set the mood, a typical evening will begin with aperitif and panatela. Usually there are three featured cigars, the first of these served directly after the main course. It is always the mildest, and smoking is permitted for 10 to 15 minutes, at which time a small savory dish is served to freshen the mouth and kill the taste of the cigar.

"Doing it this way creates the formality of putting the cigar down and prepares the tastebuds for the second," says Toby Brocklehurst, who holds frequent cigar dinners in addition to arranging cigar tours to Cuba with his company, Special Places. "You have to do this, otherwise people just keep on smoking and never get to the others."

The second cigar, often a robusto size and of medium to full strength, is accompanied by cheese and crackers and coffee. A quarter of an hour is usually long enough for appreciation, whereupon something sweet—a sorbet—is served to freshen the palate once more in preparation for the third and final cigar of the evening—always something a bit special. I attended one of Toby's dinners in Havana where he rounded off the evening with a Sancho Panza Sanchos, a mild, delicious, gentle giant, coming in at a hefty 9¼in. with a 47 ring gauge. It kept me going until the early hours.

"The emphasis is upon tasting," says Simon Chase, of U.K. cigar importers Hunters & Frankau. Chase is generally credited with designing the framework for the modern cigar dinners with chef Anton Mossiman.

"At cigar dinners in the U.S.A., as many as six cigars are smoked in an evening. In the U.K. we smoke less, and then only after good food and good wine, and in good company," he says.

Tom Conran's cigar dinners at The Cow, in London's Notting Hill, attract a fashionable crowd of thirtysomethings (combat fatigues, T-shirts, and sneakers, next to designer suits and tousled hair), and his presentation of the cigars is just as nonconformist. First up are a Hoyo de Monterrey Epicure No. 1 and Cohiba Siglo IV (voted one and five respectively in a *Cigar Aficionado* blind tasting of 94 corona gordas). The third cigar, another Hoyo, the Epicure No. 2, is his father's personal favorite.

"Dig in," says Tom breaking with convention and opening all three boxes.

Chef Caroline Perry prepared a hearty feast commencing with terrine of pancetta, foie gras, and liver with red onion marmalade. A choice of roast guinea fowl in rosemary salt crust or bouillabaisse with langoustines, crab, mussels and saffron aioli. The meal was rounded off with cheese and apple and celery chutney, followed by tarte tatin.

The wines a Californian chardonnay, an Australian shiraz and a French white Graves.

Dinner at Tom Conran's The Cow.
Hoyo de Monterrey Epicures Nos. 1 and 2
and a Cohiba Siglo IV: bon appétit.

# Cigar colors

Cigars come in seven very distinctive wrapper leaf shades, from pale green to almost black. Generally, the longer the leaf remains on the plant the darker and sweeter it is, although not necessarily the stronger. Wrapper leaves are grown in Brazil, Cameroon, Cuba, the Dominican Republic, Ecuador, Honduras, Nicaragua, Sumatra, and the United States.
The six basic shades are:

**Double Claro:** light green to yellow, heated artificially to fix the chlorophyll and increase sugar content.

**Claro:** blond, milky brown with minimal flavor.

**Colorado Claro:** Tawny, mid-brown, and aromatic.

**Colorado:** The classic, grown-in-the-shade, medium brown wrapper with a rich flavor.

**Colorado Maduro:** A ripe, more intense brown, with a full flavor.

**Maduro:** Mature, dark, yet often a mild, sweet wrapper with an oily texture.

**Oscuro:** Dark, almost black as a result of being on the plant the longest.

# Cigar shapes & sizes

Unfortunately for the novice there is no easy guide to shapes and sizes. There are over 40 basic Cuban sizes alone and literally hundreds if you include those from other countries.

Cuban sizes range from under 4in. to 9in. in length, with girths or ring gauges—measured in 64ths of an inch—from 26 to 52. However, complicating matters are the manufacturers who use the same names (panatela, corona, etc.) but cannot agree on their respective sizes. So, for example, a Romeo y Julieta panatela measures 4⅝in. x 34 and a Cohiba 4½in. x 26.

It is best to use one of the core nine shapes as a starting block. Since they are widely recognized by all manufacturers, any salesperson will know what you are talking about. They are:

| | |
|---|---|
| petit corona | 4in. x 40/42 |
| panatela | 5in.-7½in. x 26-38 |
| londsdale | 6¾in. x 42/44 |
| corona | 5½in. x 42 |
| corona gorda | 5⅝in. x 46 |
| double corona | 7½in. x 49 |
| robusto | 4⅞in x 50 |
| churchill | 7in. x 47 |
| figurado | any size |

Figurado, tapered at one end, may be called pyramid, belicoso, or semi-figurado. The French have their own word, *obus*, meaning canon shell. Those tapered at both ends become figurado or perfecto. However, both are often referred to, rightly or wrongly, as torpedoes. The strangest are *culebra* (pictured left)—three panatelas twisted together and tied with ribbon. Traditionally these were given to cigar rollers in the factories, as a perk. Untied and smoked individually, they did become quite fashionable among avid enthusiasts.

# How to smoke a stogie

1. Select a cigar that is slightly springy to the touch, and, unless you want to make a fool of yourself, don't put it to your ear—cigars have nothing to say.
2. Remove the closed/capped end; be careful not to unravel the wrapper leaf. Blacken the other end with a match or gas flame. When it is totally charred, stick the other end in your mouth and light, turning all the time to attain an even glow.
3. Cigars are best enjoyed indoors. Only smoke after a meal, with something to drink, and under no circumstances inhale. Savor the smoke, allowing it to circulate, and take your time: a cigar smoked correctly spends longer away from the mouth than in it.
4. Allow the ash to fall off in its own time and don't panic if it goes out. Simply clean the end with match and relight.

# clubbing

## Davidoff
5 St. James's
Street.
tel: 0171 930 3079
fax: 0171 930 5887
A corner store for
all cigar smokers'
needs, operated
with panache by
Edward Sahakian.

## W. Thurgood
161 Salisbury
House.
tel: 0171 628 5437
fax: 0171 930 5887
A firm favorite in
the City where
high-rollers know
how to celebrate—
with a Havana from
this century-old
store, of course.

## Havana Club
165 Sloane Street.
tel: 0171 245 0890
fax: 0171 245 0895
Smart retail
appendage to Monty's
—the elegant
members' club next
door.

## James J. Fox and
## Robert Lewis
19 St. James's
Street.
tel: 0171 930 3787
fax: 0171 495 0097
Tom Cruise and
Harvey Keitel store
their stogies at
this 200-year-old
tobacconist. The
young Winston
Churchill opened a
cigar account here
upon being elected
member of parliament
in 1900. You can
even light up and
relax in the great
man's favorite
leather chair.

## Bibendum (2)
Michelin House,
81 Fulham Road.
tel: 0171 581 5817
fax: 0171 823 7925
The flagship
restaurant of Sir
Terence Conran (1)
has the cigar-
smoking, pneumatic
bon viveur,
Bibendum, as its
symbol and *Nunc
est Bibendum*
("Now is the time
to drink") as its
motto.

## The Leopard Lounge,
The Broadway, 474
Fulham Road.
tel: 0171 385 0834
fax: 0171 385 0862
Glam 70s disco
every Thurs., Fri.,
and Sat. night, run
by cigar smokers
Alexis Billson and
Howard Spooner (4).

## Sautter of Mayfair
106 Mount Street.
tel/fax: 0171 499
4866
A benchmark retailer
located in a fine
Victorian gothic
town house in
Mayfair. Good
advice and a range
of paraphernalia.

## Shervingtons Cigar
## Merchants
337/338 High
Holborn.
tel: 0171 405 2929
Bags of Old World
character in this
mock Tudor store,
depicted on the
label of Old
Holborn tobacco and
close to the site
of the original
factory.

## Che
23-26 St. James's
Street.
tel: 0171 747 9380
Serious aficionados
Michael Naylor-
Leyland, John Beech,
and Hani Farsi (3)
bring a touch of
New York to the
West End.

2

3

1

4

The Cow
89 Westbourne Park
Road.
tel: 0171 221 5400
fax: 0171 221 7717
Tom Conran (5)
offers oysters and
stout downstairs;
occasional cigar
dinners, for
sophisticated
Notting Hill
bohemians, upstairs.

5

TomTom Cigars
63 Elizabeth
Street.
Tel: 0171 730 1790
fax: 0171 730 1816
www.tomtom.co.uk
Owner Tom Assheton
takes a fresh,
modern, design-led
approach with the
capital's coolest
cigar store. All
the familiar labels
and expertise—but
better dressed.

No. 1 Cigar Club
1 Percy Street.
tel: 0171 636 8141
fax: 0171 636 2826
Open for just a
year and already
*Cigar Aficionado*
editor and publisher,
Marvin Shanken, has
a humidor in the
first-floor bar.
A sympathetically
renovated town
house with a Cuban
theme, open to non-
members before
11 p.m.

London

**A La Civette**
157 Rue Saint-
Honoré.
tel: 01 42 96 04 99
fax: 01 42 60 44 78
Recently refurbished,
now featuring a
walk-in humidor, this
Davidoff franchise
has been supplying
Parisians with
Havanas for over
200 years.

**La Tabatière**
17 Boulevard
Montmartre.
tel/fax: 01 42 96 55
94
Informal
tobacconist for
locals who tend to
buy in ones and
twos, lunchtimes,
and after work. An
excellent stock of
Dominicans for the
scooter-riding
crowd.

**Tabac George V**
22 Avenue George V
tel: 01 47 23 44 75
fax: 01 47 23 84 82
A good selection of
pristine Cubans
(that's saying
something), humidors
and the biggest
range of cutters I
came across on my
travels.

**Bar Ducasse (1)**
59 Avenue Raymond-
Poincaré.
tel: 01 47 27 12 27
fax: 01 47 27 31 22
Premier chef Alain
Ducasse has added
another dimension
to his modern
interpretation of
classic French
cuisine, within
this exquisite, Art
Nouveau town house:
an English-style
cigar lounge. There
is a long and
tempting selection
of vintage cognacs
and armagnacs (3)
and an imposing
pair of glass
pyramid humidors,
stocked with all
the best and
biggest Havanas.

**Le Fumoir (2 & 4)**
Place du Louvre,
6 Rue de l'Amiral-
Coligny.
tel: 01 42 92 00 24
Although I was
reprimanded by two
non-smokers who had
not grasped the
meaning of *fumoir*,
this is a safe
haven for cigars.
It has a cool
conversational
crowd and a library
at the back.

# paris

**Cape et Volute**
3 Cité de Varenne.
tel: 01 45 44 05 89
A women-only cigar
club, run by
president Valerie
Kerever (5), with
frequent and well-
attended dinners.

**Cubana (7)**
47 Rue Vavin.
tel: 01 40 46 80 81
fax: 01 40 46 98 00
Cuban-themed
bar/restaurants are
opening all the
time in Paris. This
excellent one, in
the heart of late-
night Montparnasse,
has the distinction
of serving the best
mojitos (rum and
lime cocktails)
outside of Havana
and is notable for
its Cuban staff.

**Hemingway Bar**
The Ritz Hotel,
15 Place Vendome.
tel: 01 43 16 30 30
A small, intimate,
and surprisingly
local bar, tucked
away at the back
of the hotel. Colin
Field (8), the
English barman,
will design a
cocktail for every
mood and cigar (see
The Knowledge, page
171).

**La Casa del Habano**
169 Boulevard
Saint-Germain.
tel: 01 45 49 24 30
Jack Nicholson was
paparazzi-snapped
leaving here with
a handful of Cuban
cigars. I think he
should have lit one
and stuck around and
enjoyed the artistic
ambience of the
downstairs bar and
bistro (6 & 9).

**De La Concha (1)**
1390 Avenue of the Americas, Manhattan.
tel: 212 757 3167
Lionel Melendi is Cuban and his father, who founded the business, was a master tobacco blender. With a recent doubling of its retail space, this hectic, fun, uptown institution is "a zoo" on weekends, says the boss.

**J.R. Cigars (2 & 3)**
11 East 45th Street, Manhattan.
tel: 212 983 4160
Pile 'em high and sell 'em cheap. Good-value cigars and paraphernalia for aficionados, including owner Lew Rothman (2), who can live without the frills. Meanwhile, the Whippany head office boasts the largest walk-in humidor in the world.

**Nat Sherman International**
500 Fifth Avenue, Manhattan.
tel: 212 764 5000
fax: 212 246 8639
Classy smoking institution, notable for a range of cigars named after Big Apple icons: City Desk, Gotham, Manhattan, etc. Light up and enjoy the piano lounge upstairs and Nat's collection of cigar memorabilia.

1

2

3

4

**Bars & Books (4)**
889 First Avenue, Manhattan.
tel: 212 980 9476
fax: 212 980 9483
007 has lit up in the cozy back room and Mel Gibson was turned away for not wearing a jacket, but that's showbusiness. An elegant, intimate den of all things nice. One of the first of a chain of relaxed, New York cigar bars.

Cibar
56 Irving Place,
Manhattan.
tel: 212 460 5656
fax: 212 460 0011
Beneath the discreet
Inn at Irving Place
Hotel, Cibar is one
of my favorite
places to unwind,
featuring the best
of modern chic,
evoked by waitress
Martha Millan (5),
dynamite vodka
martinis, a terrace,
and well-maintained
humidor. Be warned
though, anything
smaller than a
robusto and you'll
feel underdressed.

**Club Macanudo**
26 East 63rd Street,
Manhattan.
tel: 212 752 8200
fax: 212 752 7770
Everyone I met said
I had to see this
gentlemanly,
open-to-the-public
"club." High rollers
and movie stars have
humidors here and
if you wear chinos
and a confident
smile you will not
feel out of place.

**Four Seasons Hotel**
57 East 57th Street,
Manhattan.
tel: 212 758 5700
fax: 212 758 5711/17
The Fifty-Seven
Fifty-Seven Bar (1),
with a 22-foot-high
ceiling and
sophisticated air-
extraction system,
is one of *the* places
for Friday night
aficionados.

**Havana Tea Room
Cigar House (2)**
265 East 78th
Street,
Manhattan.
tel: 212 327 2012
Eccentric, delight-
ful, theatrical,
Cuban, tranquil,
seductive. Hot tea,
and cigars wrapped
up in satin ribbon
in *fin de siècle*
glass cabinets.
Owner Jeff Tass has
a penchant for black
velvet and enjoys
his cigars with a
minimum of fuss.

**Patroon**
160 East 46th Street,
Manhattan.
tel: 212 883 7373
fax: 212 883 1118
The glass-paneled
and louvered up-
stairs cigar lounge
is reminiscent of a
1930s ships' cabin
and the brass-
padlocked, wire-
mesh members'
humidors reveal a
collective fondness
for Cuba's
forbidden fruit.
The extensive
Dominican cigar
list includes those
fabulous Moore &
Bode torpedoes from
Miami.

**Pravda**
281 Lafayette Street,
Manhattan.
tel: 212 226 4696
Seductive, late-
night, subterranean
speakeasy, with old
leather furniture
and a feel of old
Russia. Eugene (3)
attends to cigars
(see Burning Desire
page 138) which the
more heretical
customers wash down
with vodka.

new york

## Grand Havana House of Cigars

North Canon Drive, Beverly Hills.
tel: 310 385 7700
fax: 310 385 0139
Small yet well-stocked corner shop, directly below the famed club of the same name. Strong links with the Arturo Fuente family, in the Dominican Republic, ensure a steady flow of top-notch cigars.

## Kramers

9531 Little Santa Monica, Beverly Hills.
tel: 310 273 9777
Mrs. Kramer is not impressed by the fashion for cigars (she practically threw me out) and definitely does not enjoy being a tourist attraction. It is worth being barked at, though, for her display of pre-Castro Havanas, the faded press cuttings, and other bits of Los Angeles cigar-related memorabilia.

## Beverly Hills Pipe & Tobacco Company

218 North Beverly, Beverly Hills.
tel: 310 276 7358
Quirky and eccentric. There is a range of paraphernalia, old and new, and a small but interesting range of well-priced cigars in the small, walk-in humidor.

## Up In Smoke

8278 Santa Monica, Hollywood.
tel: 213 654 8173.
Locals call this a cigar divan, but it is really a shop with a counter to lean on and a scattering of stools. A good place to unwind and investigate top brands from the Dominican Republic (rare Arturo Fuente Hemingway Short Stories) and Honduras. Jeans and sneakers and you feel overdressed!

1

## Big Easy—a cigar sanctuary

1922 Westwood Boulevard, Westwood.
tel: 310 234 3279
The neon cousin of the original Big Easy in Studio City: a big, airy, friendly cigar hangout, with leather furniture, books, cold drinks, and even a pinball machine. A place for an after-work smoke and read. And how about the large bottle of mouthwash in the restrooms for customer service?

## Wally's Cigar Box

2107 Westwood Boulevard, Westwood.
tel: 310 475 0606
fax: 310 475 1450
A natural development of the wine merchants next door, Wally's has the distinction of being the only shop, to my knowledge, actually built to look like a cigar box. Among a bewildering array of styles and blends the Rafael (large size only) is their own.

## Grand Havana Room

310 North Canon Drive, Beverly Hills.
tel: 310 247 2900
fax: 310 474 7475
This big L.A. pose is rife with stories of Hollywood stars having journalists and film crews tossed out. There is an impressive, curved humidor room (1), behind a wall of glass, although when I visited the waitresses did not appear to know one cigar from another. It's related to the original Grand Havana Room in New York (and thus with more showbiz members than a Palm Springs golf tournament), so we can expect this benchmark lounge to sire many equally exclusive offspring.

**Cigar Connection**
534 Lincoln Road,
South Beach.
tel: 305 531 7373
fax: 305 531 0501
It is boom time for
cigars along
pedestrianized
Lincoln Road. Cigar
Connection was one
of the first and is
one of the best,
too. Rosie sits in
the window and
rolls, and inside
there is a wide
selection of their
own Panamanian and
flavored cigars, for
fashionable South
Beach aesthetes.

**South Beach News &
Tobacco**
710 Washington
Avenue,
South Beach.
tel: 305 673 3002
fax: 305 532 1004
From its beginnings
as a local
tobacconist, this
has developed into
a fully fledged
cigar divan, with
a branch on Lincoln
Road.

**El Credito (4)**
1106 South West
Eighth Street.
tel: 305 858 4162
In the heart of
Little Havana, with
the scent of freshly
roasted coffee on
the breeze, El Credito
is a must. There is
a shop counter
inside the cigar-
rolling *galera*.
Don't expect anyone
to speak English or
to help you choose.
Be decisive and
grab a handful of
excellent Cuban
seed cigars.

**Babalus (6)**
500 Espanola Way,
South Beach.
tel: 305 538 0679
Funky and informal
—a sort of Cuban
cultural center and
bric-a-brac store
for music and cigar
lovers. Their own
blend is rolled on
the premises.

**Cigars Under The
Stars**
Biltmore Hotel,
1200 Anastasia
Avenue,
Coral Gables.
tel: 305 445 1926
fax: 305 913 3159
A Friday night
institution on the
top floor of Miami's
most distinguished
hotel.

**Victor's Cafe**
2340 South West
32nd Street,
Miami.
tel: 305 445 1313
fax: 305 445 2372
My favorite Cuban
restaurant in Miami
has a cocktail
lounge and cabaret.
Cigars are as de
rigueur as
traditional Cuban
*guayabera* shirts.

5

6

7

9

**News Cafe (1)**
800 Ocean Drive,
South Beach.
tel: 305 532 4550
Not a cigar club or
divan per se, but
nevertheless a
popular place to
sit, smoke, and
people-watch.

**The Living Room
at The Strand
(2, 3, 5, 7-9)**
671 Washington
Avenue, South Beach.
tel: 305 532 2340
The hippest place
on South Beach, red
velvet drapes and *fin
de siècle* furniture.
This is a late-
night refuge for
beautiful night-owls
and the site of the
world's first
cigar-dispensing
machine.

8

club

Rehearsals for Club Tropicana in
Havana, and the air is heavy
with the scent of perspiration
and tobacco. Back from their
European tour, the 80 or so singers
and dancers, in their daywear,
stripped of their sequinned
costumes and feather-boa
headgear, are working on new
routines for what is the world's
longest running cabaret. The
spicy confection of mulatto
beauties and salsa started nearly
six decades ago, and the
graffiti on the walls of its
Bodegita Bar bear witness to
those—including Ernest Hemingway,
of course—who have succumbed to
its exotic, syncopated rhythms.
Today they look like regular
Cubans, albeit with
exceptionally long legs, but
tonight—they will shine.

186 clubbing

tropicana

# havana

**Casa del Habano (1 & 2)**
Fabrica Partagas,
Industria, No. 520
Old Havana.
tel: 537 33 80 60
Every aficionado
winds up here
eventually. There
is an impressive
selection and an
inviting back bar.
Look like a high
roller, and relax.

**Casa del Tabaco**
Hostel Valencia,
Calle Oficios
No. 53,
Old Havana.
tel: 537 62 38 01.
A small, traditional
cigar shop, set in
the courtyard of a
Spanish, colonial-
style hostel, shaded
by foliage. There
is a good selection
of cigars on show,
but chat with the
staff and they may
be coaxed into
producing the
really good stuff.

**Casa del Habano**
Hemingway Marina,
Quinta Playa.
tel: 537 24 11 51
(ext. 2875)
Supplied directly
by Habanos, but not
as well-known and
therefore carrying
a much bigger stock
and range.

**El Floridita**                    1
Obispo No. 557.
Walk in the footsteps
of Ernest Hemingway
at Havana's most
celebrated bar.
Renovated but still
packed and a classic
place to smoke.

**Le Select**                       2
Club de Cuba,
Calle 28,
Miramar.
tel: 537 24 10 11
Affiliated to the
No. 1 Cigar Club in
London. There is
a garden, pool, a
gym, and lunchtime
fashion show.
Members-only, but
invited guests are
welcome.

**La Veranda (3)**                  3
Hotel Nacional de
Cuba,
21, Vedado.
tel: 537 33 35 64
fax: 537 33 50 54
Arranged along walls
overlooking the
ocean, this is simply
one of the best bars
in the world. There
is a cigar shop
downstairs and the
mojitos are the best.

**The Cohiba Cigar Divan**
Mandarin Hotel,
Hong Kong.
tel: 852 2522 0111
fax: 852 2520 6528
A Cuban ambience for this club, owned by David Tang, Asia's leading cigar distributor.

**Cheroots Club(1)**
33 Jalan Sri Hartamas 7,
Sri Hartamas,
50480 Kuala Lumpur, Malaysia.
tel: 603 653 1633
fax: 603 653 1577
Owner Jeanette Lee wanted to break with the conventional idea of a leather and wood cigar club and contacted London-based architects GAS-KL for a solution. A striking, double-height glass construction is the result, with humidor and cigar shop incorporated into the frosted glass entrance. Central to the overall effect is a 650-foot fiberoptic lighting strip, creating the illusion of smoke. Cheroots is open to the public, with an intimate members' lounge and restaurant on the first floor.

1

**Gimeno**
Ramblas de les Flors, 100,
Barcelona.
tel: 34 18 49 47
The oldest and best cigar store in the city, affiliated to the city's Epicur cigar club. Specializes in Havanas in addition to a full range of Davidoffs.

**Expenduria de Tabacos**
No. 218
Calle Magallanes 16, Madrid.
tel: 34 14 48 33 45
fax: 34 14 46 28 17
The most famous of Madrid cigar stores is basically one large walk-in humidor; well stocked with an interesting and diverse selection from Cuba and the Dominican Republic, plus a full range of Spanish blends.

**Casa Central del Tabaco**
Alcala, 44,
Madrid.
tel: 34 15 21 04 20
fax: 34 15 31 05 21
This impressive, modernist emporium is the retail wing of the Spanish tobacco corporation, Tabacalera. The historical links with Havana mean there is always an excellent selection and expert staff are on hand to educate newcomers.

**Expenduria No. 74**
Barquillo, 22,
Madrid.
tel/fax:
34 15 22 02 22
A traditional store where the operators, mother and son, place the emphasis on personal service.

**"El Club'—de Sigarro Puro Habano**
Calle Serrano, 85.
Madrid.
tel: 34 15 63 76 75
Opened in 1997, a cigar club with members' humidors and a renowned, traditional Spanish restaurant.

**Club Epicur de Fumadores de Puros**
Balmes 172, 1º 2ª,
Barcelona.
tel: 3493 217 30 52
fax: 3493 217 66 84
Frequent cigar dinners and events at different locations and over 500 members at affiliated clubs in seven Spanish cities.

AUTHOR'S ACKNOWLEDGMENTS

People:
Simon Chase, Hunters & Frankau,
London.
Edward Sahakian, Davidoff,
London.
Toby Brocklehurst, Special
Places (Cigar Tours of Cuba),
East Sussex.
Kim Denman at Goddess, Los
Angeles (cover stylist).
Paul Denman, Los Angeles.
Stuart Matthewman, New York.
Versa Manos Publicity, Los Angeles.
Lew Rothman, J.R. Cigars,
Whippany, New Jersey.
Fabian "Fabs" Reyes (our man
in Havana, and team snapper).
Bruno Deffous & Gigi Letts
(our French connections).

Books:
The Cigar Companion, by Anwer
Bati & Simon Chase (Apple).
Le Morane Guide Annuel du Cigare.
The Havana Cigar, by Iain
Crawford (Hunters & Frankau).
The Connoisseurs' Book of the
Cigar by Zino Davidoff
(McGraw-Hill).
The Cigar, by Barnaby Conrad
III (Chronicle).
Holy Smoke, by G. Gabrera
Infante (Faber & Faber).

Magazines:
Cigar Aficionado, M. Shanken
Communications Inc., New York.
Smoke, Lockwood Publications,
New York.
Cigar World, Hunters &
Frankau, London.
L'Amateur de Cigare, Paris.

Quotations:
Jack Nicholson, from Cigar
Aficionado article by Arthur
Marx, Summer 1995. Copyright
© Cigar Aficionado. All
rights reserved.
Arnold Schwarzenegger, from Cigar
Aficionado article by David Shaw,
Summer 1996. Copyright © Cigar
Aficionado. All rights reserved.

Others:
Habanos, Cuba. Virgin Holidays.
American Airlines. National
Hotel, South Beach, Miami.


PHOTOGRAPHER'S
ACKNOWLEDGMENTS

Melvin Cambettie Davies at
Master Mono for his superb
black & white prints and
his insight and guidance over
the years.

The boys at Metro, Clerkenwell
Road—with special thanks to

Brian O'Leary for his
exceptional color prints.

Sang Choy International,
for their excellent color
reproduction.

Personal thanks to my
husband, Neil, for all his
support and love. I couldn't
have got through this without
you! And our little boy
Billy, for going without when
the going got tough and for
allowing himself to be bribed
with chocolate cigars.


LB PUBLISHING
ACKNOWLEDGMENTS

There are many people to
thank for helping to get this
project up and running:

- Sir Terence Conran, for
being so encouraging with our
initial synopsis, steering us
in the right direction.
- Everyone at Conran Octopus
Books, especially
Commissioning Editor Denny
Hemming, for breaking away
from the mold and giving us
the chance to produce this
project; Managing Editor
Catriona Woodburn for her
meticulous overseeing and
managing to stay sane; and
Production Manager Julian
Deeming, a true gentleman,
who saw the proofs through to
a superb standard.
- Jonathan Futrell, for his
original inspiration.
- Lucy Gowans, not only a
design guru but a dear friend
and so inspiring to work with.
- Hilary Burden, for keeping
her steely eye over this
project, & seeing everything
through on an even keel.
- Christina Wilson, our
taskmaster.
- Cheryl Newman, who
assembled an incredible cast
of famous cigar smokers with
such enthusiasm and
dedication.
- Anthony Jayes, for his
wisdom and invaluable advice.
- And the many people who
have helped and supported all
along the way—thanks guys:
Leslie, Seth, Dixie, Dani,
Daisy, Georgia, Jason, Sean,
Kelledy, Spiney, Ian, & Kim.


The Publisher thanks the
following photographers and
organizations for their kind
permission to reproduce the

photographs in this book:
Page 6 Helmut Newton/
Maconochie Photography; 80-81
Andrew Macpherson/Outline/Katz
Pictures; 83 Nicolas
Tikhomiroff/Magnum; 84 Robert
Capa/Magnum; 87 & 89 Philippe
Halsman/Magnum;
91 PEA/Kobal; 93 Photo
Snowdon/Camera Press;
94 Hans Wild/Life Magazine
(Time Inc/Katz); 96 Elliot
Erwitt/Magnum; 97 Joe
Schersel/Life Magazine (Time
Inc /Katz); 98 Paul
Schutzer/Katz; 100 Burt
Glinn/Magnum; 103 John
Stoddart/Katz; 104 Richard
Faulks/Katz; 105 Michael Ochs
Archives/Redferns; 106 Wayne
Masser/ Visages/Colorific;
108-109 Andre Rau/Sygma;
113 Aquarius Library.

GLOSSARY

cigarillo—small cigar,
traditionally $4\frac{1}{16}$in, ring gauge.
claro—medium-brown tobacco.
despalilladoras—leaf strippers.
divan—traditional cigar lounge.
figurado—bell-shaped cigars,
or tapered at one
or both ends.
humidor—storage case,
commonly of cedar wood,
with relative humidity
interior of 65 to
70 percent.
maduro—very dark brown
tobacco.
oscuro—black tobacco.
pilones—large piles, or
stacks, of tobacco over
3 feet high.
rezagadores—leaf
sorters/graders.
stogie—generic term
derived from cigars made
in the 19th century in
Conestoga, Pennsylvania.
tabacos—tobacco.
tapado—technique of
growing tobacco beneath
sheets of muslin.
vega—plantation.

# acknowledgments & index

never one for conventions,
Billy Boy chews the end off another Godiva
chocolate cigar—and swallows it.